DR. KEVIN LEMAN

GETTING

The Best

OUT OF
YOUR KIDS

Before They Get the Best of You

HARVEST HOUSE PUBLISHERS
Eugene, Oregon 97402

To Hannah Elizabeth Leman,
our little fourth-born who acts like a first-born!
You brighten my days and bring smiles to my heart.
You are truly a gift from God.

Just think...someday your parents will be the only ones
who show up at the P.T.A. meeting with our 'walkers'!

GETTING THE BEST OUT OF YOUR KIDS
A revised and updated edition of the book formerly titled *Parenthood Without Hassles.*

Copyright © 1992 by Harvest House Publishers, Inc.
Eugene, Oregon 97402

Library of Congress Cataloging-in-Publication Data

Leman, Kevin.
 Getting the best out of your kids : before they get the best
of you / Kevin Leman.
  Rev. ed. of: Parenthood without hassles, well almost! 1988.
  Includes bibliographical references.
  ISBN 0-89081-963-7
  1. Parenting—United States.   I. Leman, Kevin.   Parenthood without hassles,
well almost!   II. Title.
HQ755.8.L45   1992
649′.1—dc20   91-37694
                                                                              CIP

Printed in the United States of America.

Contents

1

Be a *Good* Parent
Have a *Great* Kid!

*T*his is a book written *for* parents, *by* a parent of four *great* kids. Does that mean I'm a *great* parent?

No. Not really. But then, it doesn't take great parents to turn out great kids. All it takes is *good* parents—like you.

Good, Not Perfect

Now I realize many parents live in constant fear that they're going to do something to mess up their children. They're afraid that one mistake and bam, their child will join the skinheads or the punkers. But that's not the way it works.

A *good* parent is, among other things, one who allows himself a margin of error. He realizes there is forgiveness and redemption, even if he occasionally blows it big-time. There have been times when I've failed to "practice what I preach" with regard to my own children. Sometimes I've turned my back on all the things I know, and let my emotions and impulses lead me. Yet I've always returned to the principles contained within this book, with fantastic results. Two of my kids are college age now, and the other two are rapidly heading in that direction. I'm thankful to say that all my kids have turned out great—and so can yours.

Unfortunately, though, many parents do make *constant* and *repeated* errors in parenting, with tragic results. Such was the case with a young man named John. It was many years ago, but I remember it as if it happened last week.

The clock read 10:30 P.M. when the phone rang. *Who could be calling at this time of the night?* I thought to myself. The business-like voice on the other end of the line brought heartbreaking news. John, one of my students at the University of Arizona had committed suicide. I took the necessary information from the police officer, made the calls that needed to be made, and tried to settle myself back to sleep.

I tossed and turned. At 1:45 A.M. I was still awake, staring into the dark. I kept asking myself why a 22-year-old man would take his own life, just before Christmas. Apparently it wasn't very important to be alive Christmas morning. When I received the report from the police department the next day, I had the opportunity to review the suicide note John had left. "I just couldn't measure up to the standards of this world. Perhaps in the next world I can do better. I'm sorry. John."

At that very moment I knew John was a "defeated perfectionist." No matter how hard he tried, no matter what he did, somehow he always fell short of what he thought he was supposed to be.

I wanted to see for myself how badly John had failed to "measure up to the standards of this world," so I went to the registrar's office and looked through the records. To my surprise, I discovered he was a graduating senior in a scientific field. In four years of university work, he had never received a grade lower than an A. He was about to graduate *summa cum laude*, yet he perceived himself as a failure.

Dealing with John's death was the saddest time I went through during my tenure as assistant dean of students at the university—a position that otherwise gave me a great deal of joy and satisfaction. Why would someone who had so much to offer the world, so much to live for, choose to throw his life away?

I realize questions like that have been asked again and again throughout history, and that there are no easy answers. At the same time, I have come to understand there are thousands of other people following in John's footsteps. They live with the pain of constant defeat and failure. They measure up to everybody's standards but their own.

By now you may be wondering, "But what part do parents play in a scenario such as this?" Sadly, they often play a major role in the underlying cause for such behavior. There's no question about it—perfectionists are created, not born. You have to learn to be perfectionistic. How does this happen?

First of all, children learn perfectionism through trial and error when they are very young. If in a given family one child is going to be perfectionistic, chances are good he or she will be the first-born. Why? I will discuss the first-born child in greater detail in Chapter 3, but it is sufficient to say at this point that the first-born bears the brunt of mom and dad's unfulfilled wishes and dreams.

Most parents "over-parent" with the first child. They set expectations much too high, and discipline much more strictly than with later-born children. They also call on the first-born more often than the other children when it comes to assistance with the home, and instill perfectionistic ideas regarding early experiences in school. How often have you observed something like this?

Little Kristin, age 3, sees mommy doing housework and anxiously asks what she can do to help. Mommy says, "Well, honey, right now mommy's very busy. Maybe later you can help."

Kristin whines and cries because she wants to help right now. Mommy relents and says, "Okay, Kristin, why don't you make your bed for me?" The little girl, delighted she can be mommy's helper, runs to her room and gives it her best effort. Admittedly, it doesn't look a whole lot better than it did before, but she's proud of it anyway.

Mommy comes into the room at this point and says, "Oh, Kristin, thank you for helping me. What a good girl you are."

But even as she's *saying* all these "right" things, she's *doing* the "wrong" things by smoothing out the wrinkles, fluffing the pillow, and basically re-doing everything Kristin just tried to do. The little girl hears her mother's complimentary words, but she also sees what's happening. She's no dummy. Even a 3-year-old gets the message that, "What I did wasn't good enough." How much better it would have been for mommy to leave the bed exactly the way her little girl made it.

In this situation, mom doesn't have a clue she's making her little girl feel bad. It wasn't her intention to blow out little Kristin's candle. Yet the expression on her daughter's face says that's exactly what has happened. The little girl has been left totally defeated by her mother's superior ability. It's easy to see where the defeatist rationale can come into Kristin's life: "What's the use of even trying? Mommy can do it so much better than I can." It's essential for parents to be able to *accept a child's effort*, no matter what kind of task is involved.

The Dark Side of Perfect

Now perfection per se isn't bad. My sister's father-in-law is a skilled craftsman, a cabinetmaker. I've had the opportunity to see his work in churches and homes, and it is probably as close to perfect as you could find. Many crafts-men with this kind of skill and God-given talent strive to do an excellent job. They can stand back, look at a particular project and say, "That's been a lot of work, but I've enjoyed it. It's just the way I wanted it to turn out." I can live with that kind of perfection—and so can anyone else.

An obsession with perfection, however, can lead to a tragedy I'm seeing more and more in my private psychologi-cal practice. That is, the defeated perfectionist. This person cannot accept what he does, regardless of how well he does it, and has a need to put himself down.

A craftsman who is a defeated perfectionist is never satisfied with what he's done. He may be forced by a deadline to finish a job, but even then he looks at it and says, "If only I could have kept working at it for another year or two. Then I would have been able to get it the way I *really* wanted it."

Unfortunately, I frequently see this kind of perfectionism in very young children. I have had occasion to observe as well as consult in several pre-schools, and have seen this pattern mani-fest itself in students as young as 3 or 4 years of age.

For example, suppose the teacher asks little Mary, age 3½ to cut out three circles for the bulletin board. After two seemingly successful attempts, Mary rips the circles to shreds and runs out of the room. The concerned teacher follows her and asks, "Mary, what's wrong? Your circles were so pretty. Why did you tear them up?"

"No," Mary sobs, "they weren't any good. Nothing I do is any good. Ask Tommy to cut out the circles."

Teacher and Mary return to the classroom. Teacher turns to Tommy and asks him to cut out the circles and place them on the bulletin board, which he promptly does. His circles aren't any better than Mary's. They may even be a little lopsided. But Mary doesn't see that. She is not making a realistic comparison of her circles with Tommy's. She is only demonstrating the way she feels inside, that nothing she does will ever be good enough. And so, as Tommy's circles are placed on the bulletin board, little Mary chalks up another defeat in her young life.

Children, as well as adults, often set standards so unreasonably high that they doom themselves to failure, reinforcing their perception that they are no good.

Another example: Teacher gathers her 12 pre-schoolers in a circle to play a game of Duck-Duck-Goose. Most of the children clap their hands and jump with glee. "Who's going to be the Goose?" one shouts. "Me! Me!" says another. "No, me!" another yells.

Timmy, age 4, takes a step backward, and then another. Teacher notices Timmy withdrawing, and goes over and encourages him to be a part of the game.

"Why don't you want to play?" she asks. Timmy just shrugs his shoulders. "Won't you please come and join us?" He shakes his head.

This may be just one of many instances in which young Timmy begins to develop a means of protecting himself from the fear of making a mistake, of doing or saying the wrong thing, of being embarrassed. Young children like Timmy—as well as adults—are quite capable of creating defense mechanisms to protect themselves from what they see as the overwhelming pain of being wrong or making a mistake. This can be seen in people who refuse to become involved and whose rationale might be, "Well, I can't be criticized for failing if I don't try." It can also be seen in those who delay starting tasks or who start so many different tasks they never finish any of them.

I believe many of the children in special education classes in schools across our country are perfectionists who have such a great fear of failing that they don't try at all. The inability of the school system to recognize and deal with this problem has led to the successive labeling and further failure of these young people, resulting in a great loss of human potential.

Is There a Defeated Perfectionist in Your Family?

I like to ask parents whether their children keep their bedrooms clean. The answer to that question can help determine whether or not there are indications suggesting a strong need to be perfect.

I'm not talking about keeping the room neat and clean in a general way. Don't think that your child is a defeated perfectionist just because there aren't mushrooms growing on his floor, or because he actually makes the bed each morning.

Rather, I'm talking about a child who is fastidious to a fault. If your child keeps his room looking as neat as your grandmother's parlor, there may be a problem. Children aren't supposed to be neat. That's not the way God designed them!

If you see patterns in one of your children's behaviors that make you think he may be a defeated perfectionist, or have strong tendencies in that direction, don't despair. That behavior can be changed. Being aware of it is the key.

If you want to know if your actions might be contributing toward the making of a defeated perfectionist, ask yourself the following questions:

• Suppose your son is setting the table for dinner. He puts the knives and spoons on the left-hand side of the plate, and the forks on the right-hand side. Would you:

A. Go in and switch the silverware around so everything was where it was supposed to be?

B. Tell your child he made a mistake and explain how to set the table properly.

C. Thank him for setting the table, leave things the way they are, and figure it really doesn't matter which side of the plate the silverware is on anyway?

• Your daughter proudly invites you to come and see how she has cleaned her room. You go into her room and are surprised to see she has really done a pretty good job. You notice, however, that she has failed miserably in her attempt to shine the mirror. Would you:

A. Walk over and begin wiping the smudges from the mirror?

B. Tell your daughter she did a good job, except for the mirror, and show her the proper way to use a bottle of Windex?

C. Thank her for doing such a good job, and leave it the way it is.

Honestly, how would you handle those two situations?

Now I know if you pride yourself on setting a nice table or keeping your home spotless, it's not easy to leave things a little bit messy. And I'm not talking just to the women either. Just as many fathers are guilty of "re-doing" things for their children, thus damaging their self-esteem.

The best choice in each of these situations is to leave things the way they are, and thank the child for the effort expended. Admittedly, if the child who set the table is 14 years old and you've told him 714 times that the knives and spoons go on the right and the forks go on the left, then you'd certainly be right to correct him. And if the daughter is a teenager who gave her room a half-hearted effort, then, yes, point out that she didn't do the job properly and ask her to try a little harder.

But, if we are talking about children who honestly did the best they could, then by all means compliment them. Let them feel the satisfaction of a job well done. You know how good you feel when you've done something and you know you've done it well. Your child needs and deserves to experience that same good feeling.

This is not to say that we as parents shouldn't teach our children to improve. Rather, it's all in how we approach it. Timing is crucial.

For example, suppose little Brewster calls you in to see how well he has set the table, and it looks like the aftermath of a cyclone. I suggest you make the most of it, but make a mental note to teach him, later on, the proper way to do it. The only stipulation is that your teaching session be far enough from his accomplishment that he doesn't feel put down or scolded for doing it wrong. In other words, if immediately after dinner you take him aside and show him the proper way to set the table, he is going to get the idea you didn't like the way he did it tonight. He will become discouraged.

If Mary Louise has streaked her mirror with glass cleaner, it might be a good idea to have her assist you with some cleaning in a week or two. Then you can share your "secrets" on how to get mirrors and windows extra-shiny. That way you will increase your child's self-esteem instead of diminishing it, and will enhance her abilities as well.

I am only using making the bed, setting the table and cleaning the room as examples because it is easy to illustrate in these situations how a child's self-esteem might be damaged. In reality, there are countless ways well-meaning mothers and fathers hurt their children without realizing it.

When a child is doing his best to please you, well, what more could you ask of him?

I was conducting a workshop at a rather large church when a young father asked me if he should allow his daughter to hang ornaments on the family Christmas tree. I shrugged and asked what was wrong with that.

"Well," he said, "I'm a perfectionistic person. I wondered if I should let her decorate the tree and then after she goes to sleep change the decorations so they are perfect, or not let her help at all?"

I could hardly believe what I was hearing, and everyone else in the large auditorium howled with laughter. They thought the question was hilarious. But dad wasn't laughing. He wasn't even smiling. He was perfectly serious, and I felt very sorry for his little girl. I told him so, but I doubt very much if one word from me was going to change his behavior. This kind of perfectionism is destructive in children, and often a main contributor to unhappiness in adult life.

Focus on What's Good

What do you see first when your child tries to clean his room? Do you see the way he straightened the far corner, or the mess he left in the near corner? In other words, are you quicker to focus on the positive or the negative?

I'm afraid our children receive far too many negative messages. For example little Johnny completes a 100-word spelling test in school. When he gets it back he sees "minus 8" at the top of the page, circled in red. Wouldn't it be just as easy to give him a "plus 92" instead?

If you have to admit you're often quick to see the negative, I urge you to make a commitment to look for the positive first. There will always be something you can compliment.

Any business person who has read books or taken courses on how to manage people knows the technique of "sandwich criticism"—presenting criticism with compliments on either side.

For example:

1. Johnson, I really appreciate the job you did on the Krelman contract. Great effort.

2. Unfortunately, this Smedlap deal is going to need a little bit more work. I think there may be a problem with some of these figures. Please take another look at it.

3. Thanks for your effort. And again, you're doing a really good job.

In this situation, the employee has been asked to do something over, but he's also been given two pats on the back. He doesn't feel discouraged and think, "Oh, they really think I blew it." Instead, he feels his work is appreciated, even though he knows he has to correct some mistakes on the Smedlap deal. This sort of management-style is very effective in the office and it translates easily into parent-child relationships as well.

It is also helpful to stay out of situations where parents are required to be judge and jury, evaluating their children's efforts needlessly. I am often asked, "What do you do when a child brings home a report card with a string of A's?"

I usually comment with a response like, "It's good to see, Sally, that you enjoy learning." That's appropriate because it puts the effort right on the child's shoulders and recognizes that the child put a lot of work into all those A's. And, it gets me out of a situation where I'm saying, "My, you're a good girl because you got A's." A child who brings home straight D's deserves a statement along the order of, "I'm sorry to see you don't enjoy learning more. Perhaps some day you will."

In other words, don't leave the child thinking you are proud of him only because of what he has done, or that you are displeased with him because his effort has not measured up. Your message to your children must always be one of unconditional love. You love them because they are children, plain and simple, and that's what they need to know.

Keys to Healthy Growth

1. Always assign children tasks within their ability.

It is never good to give a child a task he or she obviously can't accomplish. Some parents choose this strategy to "motivate" their children, but it often produces discouragement instead. On the other hand, not giving a child regular responsibilities within the home is just as destructive because it can breed irresponsibility.

2. Look for the positive.

We've already touched upon this. What I want to tell you now, however, is that if you seem to be locked into a power struggle with your child, experiencing one needless hassle after another, then it's time to try communication in a positive fashion. For example, "Hey, we can't go on like this forever—why don't we bury the hatchet? Why don't we stop digging up old bones and try to start anew?" Sometimes that's the only approach that will work. Don't be afraid to try making a fresh, positive start.

3. Discipline instead of punish.

I've already mentioned the importance of sandwiching criticism with compliments. It's also vital to remember that when you have to criticize your child for some reason, the criticism must be aimed at the *act* and never at the child himself. There is a great deal of difference between discipline and punishment. Discipline zeros in on the act. It is possible to be really angry at the act and yet still love the child. Punishment, on the other hand, focuses on the child. Too many children walk away with the feeling they are being singled out and punished unnecessarily.

In today's society there is too much of parents "punishing" their children, and children turning around and doing their best to "punish" their parents. It doesn't get anybody anywhere good. Here are a few of the differences between discipline and punishment.

• Punishment grows out of a desire for revenge; the aim of discipline is to teach and train.

• Punishment may be applied arbitrarily—"because I said so, that's why." Discipline is always reasoned and explained.

• Punishment is something parents do to their children; discipline should be seen as a natural consequence of a disobedient act.

• As I said, punishment takes aim at the child, but discipline takes aim at the act the child committed.

4. *Help children learn from their mistakes.*

When your children make mistakes—as they will—be practical and try to have a sense of humor. When milk is spilled at the dinner table, give your child a rag to clean it up, not a lecture. Lecturing him about something he didn't mean to do, and when he feels bad enough already, is counterproductive. Your first instinct may be to "fly off the handle," but if you'll take a deep breath or count to 10 before reacting, you'll deal with it much better. The old proverb tells the truth when it says there is no use crying over spilled milk. There's no reason to yell about it either! Perfectionists take such things much too seriously.

5. *Avoid comparisons.*

Let each child know he or she has an individual, special place in your heart. Don't compare your children by saying things like, "Why can't you be more like your sister?" or "Your brother never brought home grades this bad."

Very often, I find parents compare their children without meaning to or even realizing what they're doing. It works this way: Three-year-old Gertrude wants to show her parents she's learned how to do a somersault. She's thrilled until she hears daddy turn to mommy and say, "Remember when Gretchen did this?" Gertrude gets the message that what she has just done was already done by her bigger sister, who can do things so much better than she can anyway. She thought she had learned something special, but now feels like it was no big deal.

You can see the subtle kind of put-downs we parents may engage in without realizing it. That's one of the reasons so much of our children's behavior puzzles us. We wonder what caused it, not realizing that we are responsible.

How *Ragu* Changed a Life

Above all, parents need to curb their own perfectionistic tendencies. Let children behave as children, and don't expect them to be little adults. They aren't. In fact, I believe there are fewer things sadder than a child who is afraid or doesn't know how to act like a child.

When I think of perfection, I frequently think of a couple I worked with a few years ago—two of the most contrasting personalities I have dealt with. Karin, 36, was very much a perfectionist and a super-mother of six children. With all those ankle-biters running around the house competing for her time, she was still able to keep her home in perfect order.

In fact everything about her, including her children, was as nearly perfect as could be. Every time I saw her she looked like she could have stepped right off the cover of *Glamour* magazine.

Jack, on the other hand, looked more like he had stepped off the cover of *Outdoor Life*. He could have passed as a sheepherder without much difficulty.

The marriage between these two was very competitive. Karin would push forward and Jack would pull back or retreat. I had a very difficult time with this young couple, getting them to see they were in needless competition, and that the competition had to stop if their marriage was going to make it.

I spent a great deal of time in individual therapy with Karin, who eventually began to see her life had been a series of roadblocks—roadblocks she had put before herself that pretty much ensured she would fail. She had expectations and goals for her husband that were almost unattainable, but they provided her with the opportunity to say, "Jack, you've fallen short. You don't measure up, you're no good, and I don't like it."

We discussed the fact that even beautiful cathedrals were built one brick at a time. Karin had to start somewhere when it came to changing a lifestyle totally rooted in perfectionism. It was unrealistic to expect her to change everything overnight, but I knew we could get to where we wanted to be if we could make one small change after another.

Karin's perfectionistic attitude had even affected her relationship with God. She was a fine Christian woman, but she wanted her relationship with God to be perfect. Because there aren't many things that *are* perfect, she felt defeated in her spiritual life. God, in essence, wasn't big enough to love her, or to forgive her for her transgressions.

Finally, she made the necessary commitment to begin to change things in her life. She had told me on an earlier occasion that whenever she made a cake for her family she would always make it from scratch. When she had people over for dinner, everything had to be color-coordinated. She would go so far as to make sure the kids' clothing matched the napkins and candlesticks. She would even "iron" the davenport. The clear vinyl runner which usually greeted people at the door was removed only for these special occasions, when people actually were allowed to walk on the carpet.

Believe it or not, the breakthrough that saved Karin's marriage came in a bottle she bought at her local grocery store. No.... it wasn't some miracle elixir. It was spaghetti sauce.

Karin told me one evening with a sigh of relief, "Doctor Leman, my life changed when I reached for the *Ragu*." You see, previous to this time she made her spaghetti sauce from scratch—the same way she did everything else in her "perfect" kitchen. She had imposed such high standards for herself that the standards not only frustrated her, but led to inevitable failure. It wasn't easy to use "store-bought" sauce, but she did. That one act began a process that changed her life for the better.

To top it off, guess what? Her kids and husband like the *Ragu* spaghetti sauce even better than her own!

Exercises

• Arrange for a "family fun confession," in which all members of the family are going to share some of their most embarrassing moments. No deep dark secrets need to be shared, but try to get everyone to have a good time talking about some of the "goofs" they've made in life. This lets your children know that: a) everyone makes mistakes, b) it's all right to fail every once in awhile, and c) you can learn to laugh at your mistakes.

• During the next week, every time you catch yourself interacting with your child(ren) in a negative way that says "you don't measure up to my expectations," stop and make a note of it. Resolve to be less and less negative and more and more positive, even in cases where discipline or criticism is required.

• Get a Bible story book or a children's Bible and study with your child the story of the Apostle Peter, zeroing in on all the ways he failed: He tried to walk on water and sank; he resorted to physical violence in the Garden of Gethsemane; he denied three times that he knew Christ. And yet he became one of the greatest of all Bible heroes. Talk about the fact that Peter's many failures did not hold him back. Can you think of other "heroes" who have failed at some point in their lives? For example, Thomas Edison was considered to be "a dunce" when he was a child. Stress the fact that "nobody's perfect."

2

The Importance of Love and Discipline

*L*ittle Jodie, 18 months old, had never slept an entire night of her young life. As a matter of fact, she rarely slept longer than 30 minutes at one stretch. If mom was ironing, she might curl up with her blanket on the floor close to mom and fall asleep. Before long however, she would be up and at 'em again, going full speed. Occasionally, mom would try to catch a nap herself. Jodie would snuggle for a few minutes, but it wouldn't be long before she was awake and alert as ever, and into all the things that 18-month-old children can get into.

There wasn't too much of a problem during the daytime. It went by fairly easily—even though the little girl was quite successful when it came to keeping her mother busy. As evening fell, however, Jodie's fussing usually crescendoed. Mom and dad knew Jodie needed to get a proper amount of sleep, and daddy tried his best to see she got it. But whenever her parents put her into her room for the evening, she would cry and make excuses: Just one more story, one more glass of milk, one more blanket, and on and on.

Mom and dad, who were in their late 30s, explained to me that they had tried everything they could think of to get Jodie, who was their first-born child, to stay in bed and sleep through the night. They tried rocking her and lying down with her. Mom vividly recounted to me the times she would lie down on the floor next to Jodie's crib in an attempt to get her to sleep. But nothing worked.

When coddling didn't help, they tried the opposite approach—spanking, yelling, and taking away privileges. The difficulty with the punishment was not only that it didn't work, but it left mom and dad feeling terribly guilty.

They tried one other approach, ignoring her, but it didn't work either. When they just let her cry, she would do so for hours. Time after time mom would give in when she heard her daughter's crying go on and on and on. On numerous occasions, Jodie cried long and hard enough that she worked herself up into such an emotional state that she threw up. Needless to say, that meant more unpleasantness for her parents—who most definitely were not getting the rest they needed.

When Jodie's parents came to me, they were as close to being physical wrecks as any two people I've ever seen. At that point, we began an attempt to communicate our respect and love for Jodie by establishing the fact that she had a right to cry, to fuss, and even to throw up. We decided her parents could not be held accountable for her refusal to sleep, for her crying, or for her throwing up. By simply holding Jodie accountable for her actions (the crying and the throwing up), mom and dad were able to get Jodie to sleep all night after three successive nights. How? They allowed her to suffer the consequences of her behavior.

We all decided Jodie would be given her treat before bedtime, as well as her glass of milk, her opportunity to gather her "blankies," and her one story. The parents began to build a set routine for getting Jodie ready for bedtime, and they followed through beautifully.

We agreed that after they put their daughter to bed, they would not go into her room no matter how much she cried, fussed, or even if she threw up. That first night was no picnic, but since Jodie's parents couldn't take much more of the way things had been, they were determined to stick with our plan. Predictably, Jodie began to cry out for her parents to come get her. Dad had even fixed up a pair of earphones so his wife could listen to soothing music instead of her daughter's wailing. Still it wasn't easy for them to let their little girl cry all night, and then lie in her own vomit for hours. Yet that's exactly what they did.

Before you react by saying that sounds cruel, let me assure you it was the best thing they could have done for their daughter and for themselves. It took a great deal of courage not to rush to their daughter's side, just as they had always done before.

The second night didn't go much better as far as Jodie was concerned. Once again, she cried hysterically for several hours until vomiting. Once again, mom and dad refused to rush to her rescue. On the third night of employing our plan, Jodie began to sleep through the night. These two parents began to see that this little girl who had come to them so late in life certainly was a special jewel, but they could not let her control their lives. Prior to this, one of the mistakes they had made was to treat her as an extraordinary child who always needed mommy's and daddy's involvement. In fact, Jodie demanded this attention in a very powerful way. If her parents hadn't taken corrective action when they did, you can imagine the problems they would be having with their daughter today, several years later.

Many times what we must do to bring about corrective action in children takes the kind of commitment and courage displayed by Jodie's parents. Your children need to know that they are loved, and loved unconditionally, but they also need discipline and training. Any parent who thinks, "If I just love my children enough they'll grow up to be fine, upstanding citizens," is asking for trouble. It would be nice if it really worked that way, but life is not a Disney movie.

Reality Discipline

What Jodie's parents did when they let their daughter cry was employ a concept I call "reality discipline"—letting a child deal with the consequences of his or her actions. In Jodie's case, her action was to work herself into such a state that she threw up. The consequence of that action was spending the night lying—or sitting—in her own vomit.

In another case, I counseled a mother who was having a terrible time with her junior high school-age son. He wasn't really malicious—just irresponsible. For instance, at least twice a week he would miss the bus to school, meaning that mom would have to drive him. She was a single parent, who had a full-time job. Driving her son to school made her mornings a wreck. It was only a little over a mile-and-a-half to school, but it was out of her way, and it was an unnecessary intrusion into the time she needed for herself.

She tried getting her son out of bed earlier, but he always managed to dawdle around until the last minute. Even on the days when he caught the bus, he didn't make it with much time to spare.

What could mom do? First, she could buy her son an alarm clock and let him know it was his responsibility to get up in time every morning. Second, she could and did tell him that the next time he missed the bus he was going to walk to school.

He didn't say it, but he was probably thinking, "Yeah, right," because a couple of days later he missed the bus again.

When he came back into the house and told her, his mother said, "Well, you'd better get going then."

"What do you mean?"

"You know, walking."

"Walking?"

"I told you the next time you missed the bus you were going to have to walk, remember?"

He remembered, but he wasn't happy about it. He wanted to argue, but mom wasn't having any of it. It was nobody's fault but his own that he had missed the bus, and mom had had enough of suffering the consequences when she hadn't done any wrong.

"Well," he finally said, "are you going to write me a note?"

"A note? Why?"

"Because I'm going to be late to school and I'll get in trouble."

Without any meanness or anger in her voice, mom explained that if he got in trouble at school for being late, that was another consequence of his actions. No, she wasn't going to write him a note. She wasn't going to bail him out this time.

Needless to say, her son wasn't the happiest of campers. But he did learn a valuable lesson, and his days of missing the school bus came more and more infrequently until they disappeared altogether.

A parent who uses reality discipline is telling his child, "I love you . . . and I also respect you enough to allow you to face the consequences of your actions." Oh, yes, there are occasions when it's all right to bail your child out of a difficult situation. But if you do it again and again and again, you are definitely headed for trouble!

Do You Respect Your Children?

Love and mutual respect are the cornerstones of any good relationship between two people—whether those people are parent and child, husband and wife, brother and sister, friend and friend, or others. Unfortunately, based on the experience I've gained in working with hundreds of families, I'd have to say that very few family relationships are based on mutual respect and love.

Have you ever heard anyone say, "You can't choose your relatives, but you can choose your friends." Well, that's true. But you *can* choose to love and respect the members of your own family.

In the traditional America in which most of us grew up, there was a definite pecking order, a hierarchy in which everyone knew his or her place. Kings were better than queens, princes were better than princesses, men were better than women, whites were better than blacks, hispanics, or Asians, adults were better than children, and so on. The way we have dealt with children in traditional society has really been based upon principles of superior-inferior relationships, and not on mutual respect and love.

Please don't blame me for any of this! I didn't set up these attitudes in our society, and I'm certainly not defending them. I'm just telling you these were the prevailing attitudes for many years, and there is a residue from this sort of thinking that affects many of us today—no matter how enlightened we may consider ourselves to be. Let me give you an example from my own life.

I'll never forget my experience as a 19-year-old janitor at Tucson Medical Center. Like most 19-year-olds, I had set out to find an executive-level position that paid 20 to 30 thousand dollars a year. But eventually—after several months of looking for that prestigious and well-paying job—I settled on a janitor's position at $195 a month. Instead of sitting behind a big desk making multi-million dollar decisions, I found myself scrubbing out toilet bowls and mopping up spills in the cafeteria.

One of the things I am still reminded of today when I see janitors in public is that their uniform somehow conveys their place in society. My uniform was steel-gray color with a long-sleeved shirt, not at all well-suited for the high temperatures of Southern Arizona. One sleeve bore a shoulder patch with "Tucson Medical Center" written on it, complete with a saguaro cactus, the logo of the medical center. I could handle that okay, but the other shoulder was hard to take. It had the words "Tucson Medical Center" along the top edge and "housekeeping" along the bottom edge. In between these words were a crossed broom and mop—the symbol of my profession!

One day I was happy to realize my uniform shirt wasn't clean, so I wore a University of Arizona T-shirt to work. One of the nurses—think of Nurse Ratchet in *One Flew Over the Cuckoo's Nest* and you'll get the general picture—who had never so much as acknowledged my presence before, suddenly took an interest in me.

"Oh, do you go to the university, young man?"

I said yes I did, that I was in pre-medicine and that I was thinking of going into obstetrics and gynecology.

"Oh...well, listen, Alice had a birthday today and Gladys brought in a cake. The girls and I are going to get together in the nurses' lounge at 11:30. Would you care to join us?"

Before this time I had never been anything to this woman but a nuisance, someone who was occasionally in her way with his mops, buckets, and so forth. Now that she knew I was merely cleaning floors as a way to work my way through school, I was no longer viewed as a second-class citizen. With one quick change of shirts I had suddenly become the all-American boy.

How unfortunate that we tend to look at people in this light—that we often judge them by their professions, possessions, or physical appearance—instead of realizing that all human beings are created in the image of God and are worthy of respect and honor. It shouldn't have made any difference to that nurse if I planned to spend the rest of my life pushing a mop around the medical center, but obviously it did.

Many of us have difficulty in this area, even with those we claim to love. We have everybody placed on different levels, but the truth of the matter is that we are all of equal worth. And you can't really love somebody unless you also respect him—whether he's your child, your parent, or any other person in your life.

What does this have to do with rearing children? Well, unfortunately, most of us as parents tend to look down at our kids. We don't really mean to do it, or in most instances even realize that we do it, but we do it just the same. We convey the feeling that we consider them to be lesser people than we are.

Yes, we are older, bigger, and wiser because we've had more experience. But we are not inherently better than our children. One of the ways we send this message is by doing things for them that they could do very well themselves. As parents, we need to try to avoid doing this at all costs. Although we may be well-intentioned and want to help our children, we convey *disrespect* when we don't allow them to do for themselves as much as possible.

Even when your child has disobeyed you in some major way and has to face the consequences, you as a parent can see to it that his *dignity* is not damaged. Discipline and respect can go hand-in-hand. Please don't think for a minute that I'm saying you have to like everything your child does. It's possible to become angry—plenty angry at certain behaviors and still convey respect and love to your children. Too many moms and dads suffer from the "good-parent complex," as in, "I've got to be a super-parent. I've got to do everything for my child all the time without fail." That attitude can do a great deal of damage to you and your child.

Give Your Children a Choice

If you think back to your childhood, you'll probably see that you were brought up in a traditional home. On a cold winter morning mom might very well have fixed oatmeal or Cream of Wheat for you, right? Did you ever wonder why? Was it because she got oatmeal for breakfast when she was a kid, or "because it's good for you," or "it's a love pat for the tummy," or any one of the dozens of other reasons I've heard over the years from oatmeal-serving moms and dads? Now my intention is not to put down Cream-of-Wheat. I happen to like the stuff.

But did you ever feel your heart sink as you approached the breakfast table and saw a big bowl full of oatmeal for, say, the 28th day in a row. And you looked at mom with your best puppy-dog expression and said, "Would it be okay if maybe I just had a couple of pieces of toast and jam this morning?"

And mom said, "Absolutely not. Eat your oatmeal. It's good for you." So you sat there, staring at that bowl of oatmeal as it got lumpier and lumpier, wishing that just once mom would ask you what you wanted for breakfast.

It's too bad, but that type of parenting doesn't stop with oatmeal on a cold morning. The same parent who knows that oatmeal is good for you 28 days straight will also know what dress is good for you at 13 or 14, what boyfriend you should have at 17, which college you should attend, what your future vocation should be, and on and on it goes.

When I tell parents they need to give their children a choice, some of them don't respond very well. They tell me—sometimes with the veins in their necks bulging—that children need constant direction and guidance in *every area* of their lives. Yet these parents are usually stopped cold in their tracks when I ask them who is going to make the decision when that child becomes a teenager as to whether to engage in premarital sex, smoke pot, join a gang, or engage in other harmful behavior.

My point is that we need to provide decision-making opportunities for our children all along, so they will be prepared to make those more difficult and more crucial choices later on. Allowing children to make smaller decisions now will get them ready to make the kind of momentous decisions adult life will require of them someday.

Back to the analogy of breakfast on a cold winter morning. Three-year-old Phineus comes out of his bedroom groggy-eyed, his hair pointing in dozens of directions at once. He climbs up into his chair, looks at his oatmeal, and responds with one word: "Yuk." At this point, mom goes to the *reward* method as a means of getting her child to eat the food that's been put before him.

"Phineus, eat your oatmeal. It's good for you." "Eat your oatmeal and you'll grow up to be big and strong like your father." "Eat your oatmeal and I'll put some extra sugar on it." "Eat your oatmeal and I'll give you a quarter."

If that doesn't work (and it usually doesn't), mom can do a speedshift into the *punishment* mode. "If you don't eat that oatmeal, you're going back to your room." "Eat that oatmeal or I'll spank you," and so on.

Most of the time this turns into a battle of wills in which mom often ends up feeling guilty, like she isn't a "good mother" and gives in. Especially at the sight of a few tears.

Then there's the other kind of parent who needs to be mentioned here. This is the *permissive parent*, who fixes a different meal for everyone in the family so that nobody is unhappy. There's ham and eggs for Harold, buckwheat cakes for Susie and oatmeal for Phineus. In a situation like this, children are being taught that whatever they want can be theirs in life, especially if they make somebody else responsible. Poor mom. She's become a short-order cook and waitress!

What kind of parent should you be? One who can say to a child in the morning, "Phineus, you can have Krispy Kritters or Cheerios, it's up to you." Little Phineus says, "Krispy Kritters." Mom turning to the refrigerator gets the milk out and pours it on his bowl of cereal. And then, quite possibly, Phineus is going to say something along the lines of, "I've changed my mind. I want Cheerios."

If you retain only one principle out of this chapter, remember this. As Oscar Christensen says, "You can't recrisp a soggy Kritter." Once the choice is made, it is irreversible. That's the time when we, as parents, must hold our children accountable for the decisions they have made. By doing this we convey respect and love to our children, and are being good models for them.

Many parents argue that using reward and punishment can work. This is true. For example, if you pay a dollar a day to your child so that he'll keep his room clean, and you have $365 a year to pay him, he might very well keep it clean. But I prefer that he clean his room not because he can get some money by doing so, but because he lives there—because his room is part of the house, and because he has made the choice that a clean room is better than a messy room.

Another reason I'm wary of using rewards and punishment to get your children to do what you want is this: Kids aren't dummies. They learn very quickly how to avoid punishment and take advantage of rewards. For instance, what message does a child receive when you give him a reward so he will stop some particularly annoying behavior? He doesn't learn the behavior was wrong. Instead, he learns to behave in the same way as soon as possible so he can get another reward when he stops.

Suppose, for example, an elementary school teacher has had a particularly bad day behavior-wise with her class. Finally, she says, "Class, if you'll just be quiet for the next 10 minutes, I'll let you go five minutes early." With a bribe like that dangling in front of them, it's just about certain these unruly kids will become as quiet as a room full of librarians. But what happens the next day, when at approximately the same hour a mysterious hush comes over the classroom, followed by a raised hand and a small voice asking, "Can we leave early today?"

Teacher says, "No, you can't leave early. You know we don't leave here until the bell rings at 3 o'clock."

"But teacher... yesterday you said that if we were quiet we could go early. Today we were quiet, too, so why can't we leave early again?"

Teacher's going to have a difficult time handling this situation, and may wind up with a mini-size mutiny on her hands. What's more, some of her students may come to the conclusion that they weren't noisy enough earlier in the day to get the kind of treatment they got yesterday. They'll do their best to crank it up a notch tomorrow. Using a reward to produce proper behavior in her class may have helped teacher overcome her headache yesterday, but it's produced an even bigger headache today—and tomorrow might border on the unbelievable!

This Means War

Haim Ginott said some beautiful things about child-rearing in his books *Between Parent and Child* and *Between Parent and Teenager*. One of his observations that really made sense to me was, "Children are the enemy; gird yourself for war."[1] He went on to explain that many of us, overwhelmed with our new parental responsibilities, treat our children with kid gloves. We're afraid to do anything that smacks of the least bit of force, because we're afraid we're going to somehow damage their psyches.

I believe he's right on target, and his idea of regarding children as the enemy is an interesting concept. I think of the parents who are in the family room, trying to watch their favorite program on television. Their three children have just been put to bed.

Dad jumps about two feet off the couch when, without the slightest warning, he feels a small hand tap him on the shoulder. When he comes back down, he turns around and

1. Haim Ginott, *Between Parent and Child* (New York: Avon, 1969); *Between Parent and Teenager* (New York: Avon, 1971).

35

looks right into the eyes of Hurkimer, his youngest child. As soon as dad is able to catch his breath he asks the child what he wants.

"Well...um...um...*they* want to know if...." And he proceeds to relate the request that was given to him by his older brother and sister. Now the older siblings are smart enough to know the youngest is the least likely to get spanked, so they will always send him on their special missions. Besides that, even if he does get a spanking, who cares? It's no skin off their noses. They're not even sure they like him anyway.

What's happening here is that the enemy—the children—is trying to get the parents away from that favorite TV program. That's not good, because mom and dad need to have some time for themselves every evening after the children are in bed.

My point here is that this entire interruption has been organized from start to finish. It's all part of a plan. The kids want something, and they've thought about the best possible way to get it. They've drawn up their plan of attack just as surely as any general who's ever gone into battle.

I don't care how sweet and innocent your children look when they're tucked into beddie-bye at night. They can be pretty devious when it comes to getting what they want. Parents need to understand that.

Don't Just Talk—Act!

David, age 16, came to me with his mom for therapy several years ago. She said that on one occasion as she walked into her room, David was behind the door with a lamp cord in his hand. He put the cord around his mom's neck and pulled until she had just about lost her breath. Then he let her go, saying "Just a little longer and you wouldn't be here."

On another occasion, mom had been sound asleep when she woke up to feel someone's hands around her neck. It was David, who squeezed until she passed out, and then let go. Can you imagine living in that kind of situation? And yet the woman felt helpless and unable to change things.

I saw David and his mother for a period of about six months. During this time I learned a great deal about the boy and his family. David's father was killed when the boy was only 10 years old and his mother felt very guilty about it, even though she had no involvement in her husband's death. Mom explained that at times David was like a "playful puppy," and that he was a good boy, although he no longer went to school (he had quit a few weeks before they first came to see me). Because she couldn't handle David, she had moved out of the house and was staying with relatives. David was essentially living alone in a big house and he was as irresponsible as any 16-year-old walking the face of this earth. (And that's *plenty* irresponsible).

I was looking for something mom could do that would be completely out of character. That was what was needed, because there had to be a drastic and dramatic change in this mother-son relationship if it were ever going to become what it should be.

It became increasingly evident that mom had never laid a hand on David. So, in a session where he was not present, I suggested that the next time David acted like a "playful puppy," she get into a playful mood herself. Mainly, I told her I wanted her to haul off and smack him across the face with an open hand, telling him that things were going to be different in their house from now on. Believe me when I tell you I do not ordinarily advocate physical violence of any kind. I didn't want mom to hit him hard enough to blacken his eye or bloody his lip, just enough to get the message across that she was through putting up with his disrespect and violence. For mom's part, she wasn't sure she could do it, but she said she'd try.

A couple of days later a situation developed that was a perfect opportunity for mom to administer her slap to David's face. I was proud of her, because she whacked him pretty good. She didn't hurt him, but she certainly surprised him.

She reported to me that his eyes became as big as ping pong balls in amazement that his mother would take such action. Then he ran to his room, crying like a baby.

At that point we had begun to put mom in authority within the framework of their home. Following that, we told David he had the choice of either going to school or staying out of school. If he decided to stay out of school however, he would have to work to pay mom for his room and board. If he didn't want to go back to school, and refused to pay his mother, the only other option was to leave and fend for himself in the world. This was very difficult for his mother to tell him, but she saw the necessity of getting tough, and so she did.

Mom also got tough in that she stopped doing things for her son. Previously, for example, when he would come home late for dinner he could always count on the fact that it had been kept warm for him in the oven. Now when he came home an hour late one night and asked, "Where's my dinner?" mom said, "It's on the stove."

It was on the stove all right, on a plate, just as I had instructed her to leave it. David took one bite of his mashed potatoes and spit them out. "My dinner is cold!"

Instead of saying, "Well, if you had been here when you were supposed to..." and all those sorts of things, mom just said, "That's funny. Mine was warm and tasty."

David began to see mom was changing, as were the rules of the house. Through this kind of *action*, allowing David to experience the consequences of his choices and be-havior, mom began to turn things around. She regained the position of authority in her family. What had happened was that the cart (David) had gotten placed in front of the horse (mom), but she was now correcting the situation. David didn't become the perfect child overnight, but his behavior slowly improved. He gained renewed respect for his mother—which meant he stopped behaving like a "playful puppy"—and the situation in the home became better.

Most parents will acknowledge they love their children, but without discipline that love is incomplete. If parents don't discipline a child, they don't love him. Love and discipline go hand-in-hand. This is a biblical concept. Proverbs 3:11-12 says, "My son, do not despise the chastening of the Lord, Nor detest His correction; For whom the Lord loves He corrects, Just as a father the son in whom he delights." Every loving parent will find, sooner or later, that disciplinary action is an absolute necessity.

Being firm in your discipline does not mean, however, that you need to be authoritarian in your approach and refuse to allow your child any choices at all. At the same time, if I were going to choose between two less-than-ideal situations, I would definitely take the authoritarian parent over one who is inconsistent, wishy-washy, and never exercises discipline at all. One of the things all parents need to do is *develop consistency* within their lives. Children really do appreciate guidelines; they need to know where they stand and what's expected of them.

You may have read about the elementary school officials who decided the fence around their school's playground area was damaging to the psyche of the children. They felt the students would be happier and better able to express them-selves if the fence was removed.

Interestingly enough, when that fence was up, the children at play had scattered to every area of the playground, even to the point of climbing all over the fence. But once the fence was taken down, the kids tended to cluster together in the exact center of the area. Once the restraint of the fence was removed, the children were less creative in their play. They seemed to feel threatened instead of liberated. As long as the fence was there, they knew exactly what their limits were and they never went beyond them. With the fence removed, they were confused and bewildered.

You see, the limits you establish for your children will not harm or stifle them. Rather, those limits will help them grow. But again, it is also very beneficial to allow your child to make choices within the boundaries you have set.

Look Out! Here Comes a Tantrum

The first few months of a child's life are usually pretty smooth ones for his parents, with the exception of getting up in the middle of the night to feed the baby, change his soggy diaper, and so on. But for the first 18 months of his life, the child is relatively agreeable. Note that I didn't say he or she will be easy. There will be plenty of messes, fussiness and other irritations. Basically, however he'll be a pretty agreeable guy who wants to please his mother and father, who loves it when he sees his parents smiling.

Between 18 and 36 months however, the whole scenario changes. During this age, the child develops a sense of power.

Several years ago, when my oldest daughter Holly was at that age, we were in California on vacation. She saw a tiny tot about the same age throw one of the classic temper tantrums of all times.

She seemed to be watching this little fellow with a great deal of interest, and I assumed she was taking mental notes so she'd know what to do when she decided to throw a tantrum of her own. Also, Holly was at just the right age for a tantrum. I told my wife Sande, "Honey, Holly is going to show us a temper tantrum shortly." But, amazingly enough, we got through our week in Sacramento without one. As we began to drive home I said, "Well, I guess I was wrong—we're not going to see a temper tantrum after all."

It was just about that time that we decided to stop at a restaurant in South Lake Tahoe for breakfast. Holly apparently looked around and decided that this looked like as good a place as any to hold her "coming out" party.

She started by getting just a little bit fussy. Like many first-born children, if things weren't exactly perfect (pancakes not on the right side of the plate or something major like that), the problem could quickly take on the proportions of a major catastrophe.

As our breakfast went on, Holly became fussier and fussier, gradually working her way into a full-blown tantrum. Her display of temper reached its peak just as the manager brought a balloon in an attempt to appease her. She wasn't having any of it. Instead of accepting the balloon, she picked up the sugar container and threw it to the floor.

At that moment I exercised my parental authority, picking Holly up and marching her out of the restaurant. I placed her in the car, locked the door and went back into the restaurant.

When I got back to our table, Sande looked as if the world had ended. Tears streamed down her cheeks. She was looking out the window where she could see Holly standing in the front seat of the car, facing the restaurant, with her arms outstretched and yelling, "Mommy! Mommy!"

"Honey," Sande said, "don't you think it's time to get her?"

I looked at my watch. "Gee, hon. She's only been out there seven seconds. I think we ought to wait a little longer."

We did wait for a few minutes, in which we ate our meal in relative peace, and then we brought Holly back in to finish her breakfast. I've often thought about that scene over the years. Every time I do I am thankful it didn't happen in Tucson where I might have been recognized and people would have said, "There goes that crazy psychologist out the front door with his kid under his arm!"

Yes, even in a place where I didn't know anybody, it was difficult to discipline my child where so many people were watching—and no doubt many of them disapprovingly. But I knew the time had come for action, and so I took it.

I realize it is difficult for parents to take corrective action in public places. Believe me, children know it, too. There is a great deal of pressure on us just to smile through clenched teeth, and not do anything. Instead of taking decisive action in a situation like Holly's tantrum we tend to remind, coax, threaten, and bribe, and so we usually don't get very satisfactory results. That's why children are quick to use public places such as restaurants, shopping malls, and supermarkets to their advantage. As I mentioned earlier, when it comes to strategy, Gen. Norman Schwarzkoff has very little over the nearest 3-year-old. That's how powerful some children can be.

I mentioned it before, but I want to reiterate that there is a real difference between punishment and discipline. Punishment is directed at the child, whereas discipline is focused on the act. Therefore, it is entirely possible for parents to demonstrate their love for a child by disciplining him—and to have the child know his parents love him dearly even though they had to take corrective action. Love and discipline are not only compatible, they are *essential* for a good parent-child relationship.

Dr. Leman's Child-Care Recipe

I try to avoid recipe-like methods in dealing with children, but I do offer the following suggestions to parents:

1. Hold children accountable for their actions, at any cost.

2. Be consistent in everything you do with your children.

3. Formulate guidelines.

4. Let your children have input into those guidelines so they have a greater understanding of what is expected.

5. Be firm without dominating.

6. Use action instead of words whenever possible.

7. Don't be afraid to express your love to your child via words and hugging.

8. Put yourself in authority over your child. If there are difficulties within your family at this time and you sense things need to be turned around, start today by making some changes. Always remember you are supposed to be the one who exercises the authority in this relationship. Not only is it the right thing, it's also what God has told us as parents to do.

3

Oldest, Middle, and Youngest

I hear it all the time: "I just don't understand how our children could have turned out so differently. Betty is such a responsible person. She never gives us any trouble, and her life is really together. But that Brewster is something else. He can't make up his mind what he wants to do with his life. He's always in trouble of some sort, and I don't know what would happen if we weren't there to bail him out.

"How could this have happened? We treated our children just alike, so how could they have turned out being so different?"

My initial response is to say the first mistake these parents made was in treating all their children alike. Children in the same family can be as different as night and day, and one of the primary reasons for those differences is where they were born into the family—whether they are first-born, middle-born, or last-born children.

If you have children, I'm sure you've spent some time thinking about how very different from each other they are. Yes, it is true they will have certain characteristics in common. They may look somewhat alike, they may come up with the same expressions, make the same gestures, and so on. But there are going to be definite and deep differences in their personalities.

For instance, if you have a serious, intellectual, achieving child in your family, chances are good he is your first-born. If, in the same household, you have a rough-and-tumble, competitive yet social child, he or she is probably the one in the middle. What about the helpless child, the one who screams from one end of the house to the other, "Mom, where's my shoes?"...the one least likely to be pummeled by his parents...the one whose pet name is carried on into adult life? Yes, we're talking about the last-born, the baby in the family. Many parents with whom I've come in contact have thought about these differences, but most don't see how strongly they are connected to the child's birth order within the family.[1]

Do you remember the day your first child came into the world? Exciting, wasn't it? It was a very special day.

You had some expectations and dreams for that first-born child. Perhaps they were hopes you once had for yourself, but somehow failed to achieve. You see, first-borns are in a very difficult position in many ways, for they bear the brunt of mom and dad's unfulfilled wishes and goals. They are also in a very enviable position, however, because they receive so much of their parents' energy and attention.

Several studies of first-born children have shown they

---

1. For more information on this subject see my book *The Birth Order Book* (New York: Dell Publishing, 1985).

usually walk and talk sooner than their siblings. That is due, in large part, to the fact that parents tend to push their oldest child a little harder, expect a little more of him, and later on hold him up as a model for his younger brothers and sisters. No, it's not at all easy to be the oldest. There are a great many responsibilities that go with this position in the family. But even with all of this, the first-born child generally enjoys his place in the family. And most first-borns receive a tremendous amount of attention, not only from mom and dad, but from their grandparents as well.

Dealing with Dethronement

Let me tell you about one of the cruelest moments in the life a first-born child. He's happy as a lark, going through life singing the old song, "Life Is Just a Bowl of Cherries." Then one day, his parents announce he's going to spend a few days with grandmother and grandfather. Fine, he thinks to himself. He gets along well with those people, and figures they'll buy him a new toy or two while he's there, like they always do.

So off he goes, and has a great time. But when it comes time to go home he gets the shock of his life.

What in the world is this new "thing" that has come into his home during his absence? Mom and dad say it is a special "gift from heaven," but it doesn't look much like a gift to him. And if it did come from heaven, he wonders, why can't mommy just send it back?

I remember the parents who told me how their 4-year-old daughter reacted to the arrival of her little brother. When mom came through the door carrying him, the little girl ran over and took a long, hard look at his face.

"He's kind of wrinkled isn't he?" she asked.

"Well, honey, all little babies look like that."

The little girl shrugged and ran back to resume tea-time with her dolls.

"Well," dad asked, "what do you think of him?"

"I think we ought to get our money back," came the honest answer.

Many oldest children react in similar fashion. That's because the arrival of a younger brother or sister marks the beginning of major changes in the first-born's life. He figures his life has been pretty close to perfect up until now, and isn't exactly anxious to change things. For the very first time, he is going to be *sharing* the affection of mommy and daddy—the limelight he had enjoyed so much. But he is encouraged by his realization that even though the baby is a threat, it still cannot do all the things he can do. He's still special because he can turn somersaults and say his ABC's, because he doesn't need to wear diapers anymore, and so on.

The problems for the first-born will tend to grow as both children begin to do the same things—when the baby is no longer a baby, but begins to develop a real personality. As the second-born child grows, gains skills, and learns to talk, the competition between the two children will usually increase.

With every successive baby, the other children are affected as the makeup of the family changes. But no birth is quite as shocking as the second-born's birth seems to be to the first-born child. Many psychiatrists and psychologists term this event "dethronement."

I am often asked at seminars, "What can I do to minimize the dethronement effect?" It is difficult to answer a question such as this with a simple formula, because it requires a tremendous amount of loving care from both parents. It's not something that can be handled by doing one or two things and then getting back to life as usual. At the same time, however, I believe there *are* things parents can do to minimize the effects of dethronement.

1. *Communicate with the oldest child.*

The first-born needs to know what is happening in the life of the family, and how it is going to affect him. For example, if he knows from the very start that another child is coming into the family, but that the newborn's arrival will not mean mom and dad are going to love him any less, he will be more able to accept the baby when he or she arrives. Just talking about the fact that mommy is pregnant allows the child to experience the joy of the baby's development throughout the entire pregnancy. This may include taking a 3-year-old to the obstetrician's office and giving him the opporunity to hear the fetal heartbeat. Admittedly, there is a difference between talking about the arrival of the new baby and dealing with the reality when it comes. But talking about it openly will lessen the shock, and give the first-born a sense of anticipation as he awaits the birth. Again, this is the time to take every opportunity to reassure the first-born that when his younger brother or sister gets here, you will not love him or need him any less.

2. *Involve the oldest child.*

Many times I think that, without realizing it, parents tend to reject the older child after the birth of a newborn. They tell the child that the baby is too little to touch, too little to cuddle, too little to feed, too little to do anything with. But it is very important that the older children see they are still very much a part of the family. With parental supervision, they should be allowed to hold the baby, help feed it, or assist mom or dad when a diaper needs to be changed. If the oldest child is totally kept away from the baby, he is going to get the impression that this child is more important than he is, better than he is—that it's the most precious thing in the family.

That is not at all what you want to happen. On the other hand, allowing him to help you with the baby will help to reinforce the idea that he is still a very important member of the family.

3. *Let your first-born know you love him.*

It's important for an oldest child to understand that the additional time and energy mom and dad are investing in the new baby doesn't mean he is rejected or loved any less. This is the time when the oldest child needs to be taken out to his favorite hamburger place, or to the park for a long session on the swings or merry-go-round. He may attempt to revert to babyish behavior to get this type of attention. If he does, he doesn't need to be scolded. He needs to be loved.

For example, the oldest child may suddenly begin wetting his pants again, or talking baby talk. Admittedly, the last thing mom needs when she's got her hands full with a helpless baby is to have her oldest child start acting like a baby, too. But if this sort of thing should happen, it's better to talk to the oldest child lovingly and patiently, explaining that the baby does these things because he doesn't know any better. Assure your child that he doesn't need to do these things to get mommy and daddy's attention. Everything you say and do should be aimed at reinforcing in his mind the fact that you love him very much, you always will, and the baby's presence in the family doesn't change that one bit.

Characteristics of First-Born Children

First-born children tend to be achievers, and are often perfectionistic in at least some facet of their lives. They tend to be fearful of new situations, cautious, conscientious, and reliable. We can also predict they will conform to standards that they perceive to be required or demanded in a given situation. First-born children have high levels of expectations for themselves, and they tend to assume certain roles early within a family—roles that usually remain constant throughout the teenage years.

For example, if there's a "garbage person" in the family, it's typically the first-born child. Now before you first-born readers get angry and throw this book in the incinerator, let me explain that I did not say the first-born was a "garbagey" person. I said he was a "garbage" person. That means he's often the one who takes out the garbage.

One day, along about the time he's 6 or 7 years old, his mother says "Honey, do me a favor and take out the garbage tonight?" The little boy (or girl) obligingly does it because, like most oldest children, he wants to please his mom and dad. But what the poor little tyke doesn't know is that this isn't just a "tonight" thing, nor is it a "once-in-awhile" thing. He'll be taking out the garbage for the next 13 years, until he leaves home for college, or to get a place of his own.

Now certainly at some point in time, the job of taking out the garbage could be passed to one of his younger siblings. But that rarely happens. Once the first-born has been handed that rather inglorious job, it's his for the rest of his childhood. Now I can't think of a whole lot of things that are worse than being expected to take out the garbage every night for 13 or more years, but that's the way it is for the first-born.

First-borns tend to be "tuned in" to adult values, to be very comfortable with adults. In fact, they are very much like "little adults." If they tend to be comfortable with adults, they also tend to be quite uncomfortable around children their own ages.

Much of the first-born's difficulties center around the fact that oldest children are "guinea pigs." Mom and dad, being new at this parenting business, experiment with him. If something doesn't work, then fine. At least they know not to try it on their later children. If there are parental mistakes to be made, you can pretty much count on the first-born to bear the brunt of them. Of course, being the oldest in a family occasionally works to a child's advantage in this regard, too. When the first child comes along, mom and dad may read every book on parenting they can get their hands on so they can make sure they do this correctly. Then, when subsequent children are born, mom and dad are more relaxed—careless, even—because parenting has become "old hat." The younger children sometimes don't get the caring attention the first-born received. By and large, however, the first-born is the "crash-test dummy," and the other children in the family benefit from his experiences.

Characteristics of Middle-Born Children

Now when it comes to the second-born or middle-born child in a family, you can expect a much more comfortable relationship with mom and dad. In fact, middle-born children tend to be much more sociable all the way around. Whereas first-borns are likely to be loners, middle-borns are probably going to have many friends. Middle-borns seem to thrive within the context of the group, and really are social animals. That means, look out for peer pressure!

Another thing about middle-borns is that they will almost always strive to avoid direct opposition with their older siblings. This is true especially if the second-born child is of the same sex as the older child. I realize that right now some readers are shaking their heads and thinking that I've really missed it with this one. I can hear it now, "How can you say the first-born and second-born aren't competitive? My two are always at each other's throats!"

While that may be true, that's not really what I'm talking about. What I mean is that the second child in a family will look for a way to become his own person, to get attention and recognition in a way that is different from how the oldest gets his attention and recognition. For example, if the first-born child in a family excels in academics, the second-born is more likely to direct his energies into the arts, sports, or some other area.

When the middle child sees her older sister coming home with a report card full of A's and sees how proud mom and dad are over this accomplishment, she's going to think, "I can never compete with her. She's too smart. I know! I'll become really good at tennis!" Actually, what takes place is not reasoned out quite like that—it occurs more on the subconscious level. But that is the gist of it.

Nevertheless, it is going to be difficult for the middle-born child to get the attention he craves. To understand what I'm talking about, take a look at the family photo album of just about any family in your neighborhood. Notice the 3,000 pictures of the first-born child, bound in eight volumes. Then compare this with the 17 or so photos of the second-born scattered here and there. Here's the first-born, getting his first bike, going off for his first day at school. Here he is standing in the living room, sitting in the dining room, lying down in the bedroom, and on it goes. But where in the world is the middle-born?

It's not that the middle child is loved any less, but that the birth of the first child was an extra-special event, and that anything and everything he ever did was, too. And then when the youngest child comes along, he is treated as special because he's "the baby," and always will be, even when he's 57 years old, bald, and 240 pounds! What I'm saying is that the middle-born tends to be the anonymous child in the family. That is why he will look so hard for ways he can excel and prove himself. His relative anonymity with the family also helps explain why the peer group is so important to him. This is where he can be "somebody," and receive the attention he may feel he is not getting from his parents. Of course parents must do everything they can to make each of their children feel special, but this is especially true with the second-born.

Before I go on, I think I should explain that whereas I am using the terms "middle-born" and "second-born" interchangeably, I do understand there are many families where there are five, six, or even more children. There are a number of variables that enter into the equation, and I'll talk about some of those in just a moment. Basically, however, all children between the oldest and youngest may be considered middle-borns or second-borns. Do keep in mind, though, that as each additional child is born into the family, his personality will be affected by the personalities of his older brothers and sisters, most directly by the child immediately above him in age.

Now, what are the advantages of being the middle child? Well, first of all he has an older sibling who has served as a buffer for him, who has taught mom and dad a great deal about parenting. The middle child also has the advantage in having an older child in the family after which he can model himself, even if that modeling takes the form of "Boy, I sure don't want to be like him." For example, if the first-born child is disagreeable with mom and dad and always into hassles with them, the second-born is likely to make a real effort to get along. In fact, many studies of middle-born children have shown they have a tendency to be peacemakers or go-between. Why this is so can be understood by considering the second-born's position in the family. The middle-born can understand a little bit of what it's like to be the oldest in the family, but he can also understand a little bit of what it's like to be the youngest. He has a unique vantage point that enables him to see things from various perspectives. This often enables him to be a master negotiator.

What are some other tendencies of middle-born children? They tend to be impatient, social, aggressive, and sometimes rebellious. (Remember, the first-born wants to please his mother and father, whereas the middle-born is more anxious to please his peer group.) Middle-borns thrive on competition and tend to be much more independent than first-borns—at least where their parents are concerned.

Characteristics of Last-Born Children

If you're throwing a party and you want to have a fun and crazy time, it would be a good idea to invite a whole bunch of last-borns.

On the other hand, if you want to have a serious discussion about the economic problems facing our country, for the most part you need to stay clear of these folks.

That pretty much sums it up. Last-borns tend to be party animals who just want to have a good time. When it comes to planning for the future or tackling problem situations head on, they just don't want to hear about it. They tend to be Goodtime Charlies and Charlenes. What's more, those irresponsible but fun-loving and fun-to-be-around tendencies are likely to manifest themselves very early in a child's life.

I'm not suggesting that all last-borns are irresponsible. But I am saying they have a natural tendency to go in that direction. They can overcome this tendency and many have, but it's likely to take a concerted effort.

And, just in case it sounds like I'm being particularly hard on these "babies of the family," let me assure you I have the right. I know these people best of all. I *am* one of them.

Let's face it, the youngest child in a family is the one who is most apt to "get away with murder." He's the one who is most adept at getting other people to do things for him, and he is an expert at placing people in his service. The youngest child is in a very special place in that his birth marks the end of the trail. He also profits from having older brothers and sisters, giving him a unique opportunity to assimilate traits and skills from many people in the family and incorporate them into his personality. He has many teachers, and many examples to follow, and this may work very much to his advantage.

Youngest children tend to be experts in "setting up" older children. In other words, they create situations in which they end up being struck or yelled at by an older sibling, but then use that act as a weapon. They run to mom and dad and tell them all the bad things older brother or sister has been doing to them, and then sit back and enjoy the scolding the older child gets because he dared to lay a hand on "sweet little snookums."

Youngest children tend to be very social, very outgoing, very manipulative, and sometimes very helpless. And if you think I've used too many "very's," let me assure you I've done so on purpose. Last-borns deserve every one of those superlatives.

Characteristics of Only Children

If there is a position in the family that's worse than first-born, it's the position of the only child. "Onlies" have no sibling to relate to, and they often find their world is really an adult world, one that can impose very exacting standards. They often get the message that unless they act like little adults, they have fallen short of expectations and therefore are inadequate. There is, however, a plus on the side of only children. Overall, they tend to be very reliable and conscientious people. Not surprisingly, they tend to marry people quite a bit older than themselves, primarily because they relate so well to "older" people.

If there is a position in the family most likely to fall prey to the "defeated-perfectionist syndrome" that we talked about in chapter 1, it is probably that of the only child.

Taking a Look at the Variable

It all sounds pretty simple up to this point:

• First-born children tend to be loners, achievers, and perfectionists.

• Second-borns tend to be competitive, social, rebellious, and aggressive.

• Youngest children are generally outgoing, social, manipulative, demanding, and sometimes helpless.

• Only children tend to be adult-like and are conscientious people.

Yet while it is true that these are the general tendencies of the various birth orders, there are many variables that can affect the behavior of the individual.

Some of these variables are:

1. *Years between birth of children.*

Perhaps more than any other variable, the years between the births have a great impact on the way children develop. For example, in a family of three with a 13-year-old male, and 11-year-old female, and a 3-year-old female, we really have a "two-family" family. What that means is that because so many years have elapsed between the births of the second and third children, the youngest girl is really a family unto herself. She is, for all practical purposes, a first-born. Her brother and sister will be more like second parents or aunts and uncles than they will be siblings. I tend to use five or six years as a starting point for a new family. If there is a five or six-year gap between births, I draw a line between those two children and consider the youngest child to be a first-born rather than a last-born.

2. *The sex of the child.*

If the first two children in a family are of the same sex, they are usually opposites when it comes to personality, skills, etc. On the other hand, if they are of the opposite sex, they may develop along the same lines and the two oldest children may both have the characteristics of first-borns. It is quite possible then, for a family to have two first-borns.

3. *Physical handicaps.*

If the oldest child has a handicap of some sort, then the second child may assume the role of the first-born. This may happen because he is able to do things more quickly than his older brother or sister, or because he is forced into the role of being a caretaker and nurturer. Naturally, this often creates special problems for the child who is handicapped—who is older but perceives himself as less capable of performing the various functions and activities required by life. From time to time, you will also see a role reversal of this sort in a family where there are no handicapped children—where a younger child just develops more quickly than the older child and takes on the characteristics of the older child's place in the family.

This may especially happen in families where some of the children are adopted, and so do not share the same genetic makeup. I remember one case, for example, where the 11-year old boy was several inches taller than his 14-year-old adopted brother. The parents had a particular problem because everywhere the boys went, people asked the younger one if this was his "little brother." The older boy began developing quite an inferiority complex related to his height.

What can you do in a situation like this? Well, there's nothing you can do about the way children develop. Some just grow up faster than others. But you can alleviate problems by giving the older child additional privileges, such as a larger allowance, a later bed-time, and increased responsibilities around the house.

4. *Miscarriages.*

Another variable, that is often overlooked, is whether there have been any miscarriages. This is so primarily because the child who is born following a miscarriage is usually treated as a very special child. His or her parents have had a tragic confrontation with the fact that pregnancies don't always go well. The anguish and hurt that are associated with a miscarriage can sometimes be manifested in over-loving and making that next-born child very spoiled or pampered.

5. *Deaths.*

Obviously, deaths have a great impact upon the entire family, particularly for the child above or below the child that has passed away. If his older brother dies, the second-born son may suddenly realize he is now the oldest, and he will begin to step in and fill the shoes left empty by his brother's passing. In other words, those middle-born personality characteristics are likely to be replaced by the no-nonsense, over-achieving tendencies of the first-born.

Needless to say, whenever a family suffers the loss of a child, the event is intensely traumatic for everyone within the family. Long after the outward grieving process is ended and things get back to "normal," there are a great many painful issues that must be dealt with. Mom and dad never expected they would out-live any of their children, and there is a void in their lives that will never be filled. As for the siblings of the deceased child, there are levels of pain that go far beyond merely missing the departed brother or sister.

Given the slightest reason for doing so, children may begin thinking things like, "I'll bet mom and dad would be happier if it was me who died," and "I wonder if it's my fault that my brother died," and so on. This is definitely not an easy subject to talk about. But, it is vitally important that the grieving parents remain as open as they possibly can to their surviving children, and that they continue to deal with these children as closely as possible to the way they dealt with them before.

6. *Parents' interaction with individual children.*

This is the sixth variable that may change the "natural" birth-order roles in the family. Perhaps it is so obvious that it doesn't need to be pointed out—but I'll point it out anyway. That is, parents' interaction with their children goes a long way in forming the various personality traits that children develop. Then, once those personality traits begin to emerge, the child's parents, teachers and others tend to expect him to behave in a predictable manner—to fulfill certain roles consistent with his personality. Once a role is assumed by a child in the family, it is rarely challenged.

For example, consider the child who develops in a scholarly manner. If the child beneath the scholar in the family is of the same sex, chances are that his or her teachers are going to report, "Susie just doesn't seem to care about school. She'd rather run around, have fun, and play games than do her schoolwork."

For Susie's older sister, Sally, the teacher's report is likely to be quite different: "An absolute dream to have in the classroom. She is number one; she's on top of everything and gets straight A's."

One might assume from these reports that Susie just doesn't have what it takes to do A work. But more likely the truth is that Sally and Susie have the same capability of doing the schoolwork. Susie, however understands Sally is very well-entrenched in the position of scholar in the family, and she feels it would be impossible or too threatening to try to compete with her.

She knows, too, that her sister relates to their parents on the basis of being the scholar. For instance, mom and dad are probably going to give Sally things like books and pen-and-pencil sets for her birthday, while Susie gets a first-baseman's mitt or dolls.

Now in a typical family of four, it would be most common to find different family roles assumed by various children. For example, the scholar role could very well be assumed by the first-born child, as could the role of being mom's helper. There are countless numbers of other roles, such as: the comedian in the family, the athlete in the family, the black sheep (or as Oprah suggested to me, the white sheep), the artist, the musician, etc. As parents, we need to be very careful of the way we relate to our children—to understand the differences among them, and to look for ways to encourage and appreciate the *strengths of each* no matter what those strengths might be.

I remember one young man in his late 20's who had a difficult time dealing with people. The problem, quite honestly, was that this fellow had one rip-roaring, old-fashioned inferiority complex. It all came from the time when he was 10 or 11 years old, and his older brother was a star on the local high school sports teams. Big brother, who was nearly five years older, was an excellent performer in three sports. He was a starting tailback on the football team, an all-conference guard for the basketball team, and one of the top pitchers on the baseball team.

Mom and dad were enthusiastic boosters of the high school's sports program. They never missed a game unless it was absolutely impossible for them to be there. Dad kept a big scrapbook, crammed full of newspaper clippings detailing the on-the-field exploits of this All-American older brother.

The problem was that even though the younger brother loved sports just as much, he wasn't very good at them. On his Little League baseball team he was one of those kids who got put into the game in the last inning, just because the coach was supposed to let everyone play.

He told me he remembered lying in bed at night unable to sleep, worried about what it was going to be like for him when he got to high school. He just knew he was going to be a terrible disappointment to his parents. Beyond all of that, he had blown his brother's image up to unbelievable proportions. He figured everyone in town was just waiting for him to "blossom," so he could suddenly be as good as his brother. That way, when his brother graduated, he'd be there to take up the slack.

As time progressed, however, it became more and more apparent to him that it wasn't ever going to happen. And even though he loved sports, he decided to leave them behind. He began pouring all of his energies into academics. He won the city-wide spelling bee, and achieved some other academic awards, but of course none of those received the publicity of one of his brother's touchdown runs or 20-point basketball games. Consequently, they didn't merit a great deal of space in dad's scrapbook.

My acquaintance was struck with the feeling that he was a gigantic letdown to his parents. Even though he excelled in academics, he felt he was less-than-adequate as a human being.

He was fortunate in that with counseling help, he was able to overcome his feelings of inadequacy, at least to a major degree. His parents were fortunate also, in that he decided to put his energy into academics. What sometimes happens in a situation like this is that the child who sees himself as "not good enough" decides that if he can't be the *best* at being the *best*, he'll just have to be the *best* at being the *worst*. He begins to take on the role of "class clown" or "juvenile delinquent," or finds some other less-than-ideal way to get the recognition he wants.

The Power of Expectations

I wish I could make every parent in the world understand this principle: Children will live up or down to their parents' expectations. In my counseling experience I have dealt with many families in which one child was particularly agreeable and helpful, but another had apparently rejected the values of the family and seemed to delight in giving his or her parents as much grief as possible. Sometimes it is difficult to pinpoint a reason for this happening. Most of the time, however, it begins as a clear case of rebelling against what is perceived to be the "favoritism" enjoyed by one of the other siblings. Then, it is perpetuated as the child strives to "live down" to his parents' expectations.

I see this business of "living down to expectations" all the time, especially in public schools. In fact, I believe a student's cumulative record, which gets passed along from year to year, is the number one perpetrator of this sort of behavior.

Let's face it—once a child gets a reputation for being a troublemaker or a poor student, teachers naturally expect him to continue behaving that way. In fact, they may even respond to that child in ways that invite him to continue the undesirable behaviors.

There has been research done in which schoolteachers were given false I.Q.'s of children to see if that information would determine how they graded those students—and if changing teachers' expectations would change the way students performed in the classroom. It did.

At the end of the grading period, the children with the "highest" I.Q.'s consistently received the highest grades, while the children with the "lowest" I.Q.'s received the lowest ones—even though those I.Q. tests results were totally bogus. In fact, the truth was that the I.Q. scores had been reversed.

What was happening here? Two things. First, the teachers were undoubtedly letting their preconceptions of the children's abilities shape their perceptions of how well the children were doing in their schoolwork. Secondly, it is also likely that the children tended to "live up" or "live down" to their teachers' expectations.

I think this says an awful lot to us as parents. What do we expect from our children? Do we constantly expect them to disappoint us or let us down? If we do, that's probably what's going to happen. If, however, we expect them to make us proud and we encourage them in their various areas of strength, then they are likely to come through for us.

For example, I get so many people—mothers in particular—who tell me what happens when they babysit their friends' children. Namely, those kids are as good as gold until their mother walks into the room. Then, all of a sudden, they display their very worst manners.

Why? Because mom warned them not to misbehave, to be good. Essentially, she told them, "I expect you to misbehave." Her kids are simply behaving in a way they perceive to be expected of them.

If you don't retain much else from this book, please remember this:

Always treat a child as you expect that child to behave. If you do, you are not likely to be surprised!

Exercises

—Draw up a birth-order diagram of your family tree—not only for your children, but starting with you and your spouse. Where do you fit into your families? What tendencies from your respective birth orders can be seen in your approaches to life, and in the way you relate to each other? In your approaches to parenting? Then move on to your children, seeing if their personalities square with their birth positions. Once you have drawn up a diagram, see what conclusions can be reached with regard to the way you relate to your children. Your chart may look something like this:

Husband's Family

Cletus (husband) 34	Perfectionist, reliable
Harvey (brother) 31	Easy-going, artistic
Mary Louise (sister) 26	Manipulative, demanding

Wife's Family

Harriet (sister) 41	Conscientious, over-achiever
Annabelle (sister) 35	Independent, competitive
Yvette (wife) 31	Easy-going, "helpless"

Our Family
Dad (Cletus), Mom (Yvette)

Joshua 10	Scholarly, anxious to please
Justin 8	Rebellious, athletic
Julianna 5	Spoiled, strong-willed

Once you've built your chart, use it as a reference.

• Set aside some time over the next several weeks so that each of your children can take turns being king or queen for an evening. On that child's "big evening," let him pick out what he wants for dinner (or a restaurant for the family to go to), and after-dinner entertainment such as miniature golf, a movie, or a trip to the park. (Just make sure the dinner and entertainment are well within your family budget.) This way you are showing all of your children that you value them, and that you are not just partial to one because he's the oldest, or to another because she's the only girl, etc.

• Make a list of the strengths of your respective children. Then talk with each one about their strengths with an eye toward developing them.

Your Child's Most Important Teacher: You!

*T*wo years ago a casual acquaintance announced she was withdrawing her three children from public school, and would be teaching them at home. I knew her as a dedicated and energetic mother, and I wasn't surprised by her decision. She was joining the ranks of thousands of other parents who have decided to look into home schooling, for a variety of reasons.

Not long ago, I encountered this same woman. I hadn't seen her in awhile, so I asked how the home schooling was going. She looked down and shook her head.

"One of the biggest mistakes I've ever made!" she said. "It was much harder than I thought it would be." She went on to tell me her children were all back in school, and that she had developed a new understanding and respect for the teaching profession. Whereas this woman was once convinced there was no hope for the public schools and that the very best thing she could do was withdraw her children, she now believes public schools can be "saved" by dedicated parents working with and through them.

Having been associated with education in a number of ways myself—and having almost single-handedly driven a number of teachers to an early retirement when I was a bit younger—I can assure you teaching children is indeed a difficult and dangerous task. Now I'm not saying that many parents aren't doing an excellent job of teaching their children at home. Nor am I saying that there are a number of teachers who should have chosen other, more sedate professions—like lion taming, for instance. Rather, my experience tells me that for the most part, the men and women who are teaching our children are dedicated professionals, doing their best to educate the young people entrusted to them.

Remember the old saying, "He's somewhere between the devil and the deep blue sea"? That, to me, sums up the plight of the school teacher. He's trying to educate the children, but at the same time he's trying to please a lot of different folks.

First of all, he's got to keep the children happy. If they're not happy, the parents won't be happy either, and that will bring on some major headaches. He also has to worry about the school administration. Many teachers aren't sure their administrators will back them in the event of a conflict with parents, even if they are sure the teachers are correct. Finally, teachers have to please the school board—a group of people who are usually elected by popular vote, and who may or may not have any experience in or understanding of education.

Now it's not my purpose to write a treatise on the difficulties teachers face. But the more I hear about problems in education, the more sympathy and respect I have for the really good teachers—those doing everything within their power to see that Johnny and Judy are learning what they're supposed to be learning.

As I said, teachers often operate in an environment that is not the best or most conducive to education. Then, they have to shoulder the blame when some kid graduates from high school and barely knows the alphabet.

In my opinion, however, the biggest problem teachers face is that too many parents have the misconception that when their child begins school, he is now "the teacher's responsibility." The child will learn at school, and his parents—especially his mother—is now free to pursue hobbies, housework, and/or career.

I read recently about a young man suing the school where he received his education. Or perhaps I should say he was suing the school where he *didn't* receive his education. He's in his 20's now and has a high school diploma, but he reads at the level of a first-grader. And when it comes to math, forget it. He's totally lost. His lawsuit says the school let him down by promoting him from grade to grade and then giving him a high school diploma, even though there was no way he deserved one.

Certainly this is a tragedy. Some of the blame has to go to the teachers who, apparently, failed him. Yet my question is, didn't this boy have anybody else who cared about him? Where were his parents? Couldn't they tell he wasn't learning what he was supposed to learn? If they didn't know what was going on in their son's life, that shows an appalling lack of interest. If they did know, why didn't they try to do something about it at the time?

One of my favorite stories was told to me by Dr. Oscar Christensen, an internationally known psychologist and a colleague and friend of mine. It concerns Rufus, who came home from school with a note handwritten by his teacher:

"Dear Mrs. J.:
Rufus doesn't smell good. Please give him a bath.
Love, teacher."

Rufus' mom, a poor, uneducated black woman, wrote what I thought was a beautiful note back:

"Dear Teacher:
Rufus ain't no rose. Don't smell him. Learn him."

This story conveys where we are today with regard to education. Parents frequently point their fingers at the school, and the school points right back at the family. There is very little evidence of an effective cooperative effort between the two. This lack of cooperation only compounds the problems faced by students, their parents, and teachers.

Why Parents Are the Key

When a child goes through 12 years of school and doesn't gain enough knowledge to fill a thimble, there's enough blame for everyone—teachers and parents alike. Similarly, when a child is an excellent student with a thirst for learning, parents and teachers can usually share the credit. But when it comes to the most vital factor in determining success in education, parents have the edge. Supportive and encouraging parents can help to overcome any problems that might be caused by a bad teacher. And, we might as well face it. In 12 years of school (13 if you count kindergarten), it's pretty unlikely that a child will have all first-rate teachers.

What many parents fail to realize is that they have more opportunities than anyone else to expand the minds of their children, and to expose them to educationally enriching experiences. What parents also need to recognize is that if they rely solely on the schools to educate their children, they will certainly be disappointed.

A child may spend six or seven hours in school, five days a week. The rest of the time he's at home. In most areas, the school year runs for about 180 days. That means the child spends 185 days at home every year. Even on those days when school is in session, he spends much more time at home than in the classroom.

The home environment, more than anything else, is what shapes a young person into the adult he becomes. It is the parents' job to instill values in their child. It is their job to foster his appreciation for learning. It is their job to support him in his educational experiences so he feels good about what he's learning at school.

The Wonderful World of Books

Whenever I tell parents they need to get involved in their children's education, I am usually asked, "What can I do? I'm not a professional. I'm just a mother. How can I make my child learn?"

First of all, it's important to remember that no one— parent or teacher—can *make* a child learn. All you can do is provide experiences that will help him mature and grow. Everything you do in this regard should be designed to help your child develop an appreciation for, and take responsibility for, his own learning.

How? The first step you can take is to expose him as early as possible to the wonderful world of reading.

Incidentally, in the last chapter we talked about the differences among first-borns, middle-borns and last-borns. One of those differences is that first-borns tend to be readers. Why? Primarily because parents tend to read a great deal to their first children but then, as others come along, they just don't do it as much. This is another of the reasons first-borns tend to be scholars and achievers.

Anything you can do in the home to encourage your child's reading is invaluable. Reading is the basic skill your child must master if he is to succeed in most of his future learning. It's important to make time for reading to all your children, whether we're talking about first-born, second-born, or ninth-born.

When should you start reading to a child? Even a 6-to-9-month-old baby can be exposed to reading. Besides, it's enjoyable to cuddle your little one on your lap while the child holds the book, looks at the pictures, and listens to you pronounce the words. She may be at the age where she seems more interested in chewing on the pages than in listening to you read, but don't be discouraged. The experience is pleasurable, and helps to give her an appreciation of books even though she doesn't quite know what they're all about yet.

During pre-school years, you can help your child develop reading skills through the use of games such as picking letters out of advertisements, marquees, and billboards. Once he's learned his ABC's you can have fun playing "The Alphabet Game," especially during long trips in the car. In case you've never played it, it works like this. You compete against each other by looking for letters on billboards, highway signs, store windows, etc. First you find an A, then a B, and so on. The first one to get through the alphabet is the winner. And never fear, you can even find those hard letters like "q" on liquor stores, "x" on pedestrian and railroad X-ings, and "z" on sizes, prizes, and zoos.

There is one important rule about this game. It's for passengers only, not drivers! Perhaps you can think of other letter- or word-related games to help develop an even greater appreciation for reading.

Another thing you can do to enhance your child's reading ability is have him read to you. Chances are he will really enjoy this role reversal, especially if you show genuine interest in what he reads. One bit of advice, though: when your child stumbles over a word, you'll be tempted to immediately tell him what it is. Instead, let him try to figure it out himself. Even if he turns to you for help ask, "What does it look like to you?" Encourage him to sound it out. If he is able to figure it out, he will feel good about his accomplishment, and he'll think, "Hey, this reading is a snap!" If you really want your child to develop strong reading skills, give him an opportunity to solve his own problems. Don't let him train you to bail him out every time he's stumped. By the way, which of your children do you think will be most likely to ask for help? If you said the last-born prince or princess, give yourself 10 points!

Now if your child has tried to figure out a word but just can't seem to get it, you have at least encouraged him to use his brainpower. That's good. After a few seconds, go ahead and tell him what the word is. To let him struggle further would only frustrate him, and you don't want to do that. But don't say anything along the lines of "Come on, Alberta, you know what that word is..." or, "You can figure it out. It's *so* easy!" Comments like these make the child feel embarrassed and inadequate. Maybe you will want to have an agreement with your child that if he can't figure a word out in three tries, then you'll tell him what it is.

Another idea for encouraging your child's love of reading is to get him to share his stories with other children in the family. This is also an excellent way to involve an older child in the life of his younger brother or sister. It teaches the children to cooperate, it gives mom a break, and it encourages the younger child to be interested in reading, too.

A way you can help your child learn to read at an early age is to record his favorite stories on cassette tapes. That way, a child as young as three or four can "read" to himself as he plays the tape and looks at the words and pictures. An even younger child may memorize a book and pretend he is reading. That, too, will help instill the love of reading. And, it will provide mom and dad some relief from reading "Peter Rabbit" for the umpteenth time.

Showing interest in any book your child brings home from school is another way to encourage him to read. Pick it up. Look at it. Ask about it. If possible sit down with your child and either read the book to him or have him read it to you. It is vitally important that you always show interest in your child's reading abilities and habits. Also, remember to hold the child close, with plenty of *body contact* as you read to him. I'm convinced this type of nurturing is extremely important when it comes to developing the child's self-esteem. And, again, it helps to convey a positive feeling about reading.

Finally, there are at least two more things you can do to develop your child's interest in reading, and thus get him started on the road to success in school. First, you can take him to the library as often as possible. A small child will love to go to the library and pick out his own book because it makes him feel "big." It's a good idea to explain to the child how the library works, and introduce him to the librarian, who can help him find all sorts of interesting books. In many communities, libraries include story hours for pre-schoolers as a regular part of their programming.

Secondly, let your child see you read. As he or she sees you choose and read books yourself, you serve as a powerful model of what you hope to teach—that reading is important and enjoyable.

Putting Pencil to Paper

Another way you can be your child's best teacher is to show him the fun involved in putting words down on paper. It's generally true that reading and writing go together. A child who is used to reading words others have put on paper should be more comfortable when it comes to putting his own words on paper. But some children are flat-out stymied by writing. They're afraid of it. That inability to write can cause them many difficulties in school.

You can provide experiences to help your children begin to write as soon as they learn to print—whether it's in kindergarten or first grade.

• Use your kitchen bulletin board or chalkboard to post simple messages and directions. Urge your children to write messages to you and others in the family.

• Ask your child to print out the invitations to his next birthday party, and even help address the envelopes.

• Make sure he knows the importance of sending thank-you notes for gifts he's received.

• If your child seems to enjoy these early experiences in writing, encourage him to write a story to read to you. If he does, make sure you take the time to sit down and read it with him. Now the story may not be a masterpiece. It may be something along the lines of "Two fleas fell off the dog and hit their heads. The end." The important thing is that the child is growing and learning, and needs to be encouraged in his efforts.

Increasing Verbal Skills

You can also help your children learn the important art of verbal communication. Here are some practical ideas to consider:

• Urge them to put on plays or shows for mom and dad. You can make great memories together as you encourage your children to demonstrate their talents and abilities. Turn off the television. Have a "Family Fun Night," full of skits, songs, and other activities. This may sound a bit corny or old-fashioned, but I have a feeling families had a better idea of how to have fun together before there were TV's with 56 channels, and movie theaters on just about every corner.

If your children decide to put on a play, make sure no one feels left out. I remember our children's production of "Annie," in which Kevin II, who was 3 at the time, played the role of Annie's dog Sandy. He didn't have very many lines, but his "arf" was wonderful!

Start a story and have your child finish a sentence, or maybe even come up with the ending to the entire story. If you have more than one child in the family, the "finish the story" exercise can be great fun. You'll come up with some of the most fantastic twists and turns this side of Alfred Hitchcock.

This is how it works: Have someone start the story (yourself or one of the older children) and stop it at a particularly suspenseful part. At that point, ask somebody else to continue. This exercise not only helps each child develop language skills, but also fosters creativity.

Talk to your child—really talk to him. Show interest in what he wants to show you, and spend some time conversing with him. I've seen various studies on how much time moms and dads spend talking to their children, and it's *never more than a few minutes a day.* What a tragedy.

Believe me, I know how demanding 2- or 3-year-old children can be. They bombard their parents with a steady barrage of questions, and every answer leads to another question. I've often wondered why the Guinness Book of Records doesn't contain a section on "Most Questions Asked in a One-Hour Period by a 3-Year-Old Child." If it did, I'm sure the number would be somewhere in the thousands. In fact, my youngest daughter Hannah is passing through that stage right now, and I have thought about putting a sign out in front of my house similar to the one McDonald's uses... "40 billion asked." But as trying as it can be, it's important for the sake of the child's development that you respond as patiently and thoroughly as you can.

Now one thing you may need to know about talking with your children is that they generally don't respond well to having questions asked of them. Instead of answering, they're likely to start playing the old "buttoned-lip game."

For at least two reasons, I try to avoid asking questions about the day's happenings when my children first get home from school. For one thing, questions tend to make the child automatically defensive. Secondly, children often associate their parent's questions with having to "live up to mom and dad's standards."

The "buttoned-lip" can occur at a very young age. My sister-in-law will probably never forget her first-born son's first few days of pre-school. Picture, if you will, mom waiting for 2-year, 9-month-old Andy to come home and tell her all about it. She bubbled with anticipation. As soon as Andy got home each day, she'd start asking him what he'd learned, who he'd played with, if he liked his teacher, and so on. He'd answer her questions with nothing more than a grunt and a shrug, and run off to play.

Finally, on the fourth day, little Andy gave his mother the clincher. As he got off the school bus he told her, "Don't ask me what I learned today in pre-school, because we didn't do nothin'!"

She got the message. She backed off on her interrogations and decided he would tell her about school whenever he was ready. She didn't have to wait long.

In just a day or two, without any prodding, Andy started to share his pre-school experiences. By the end of the second week, his mom could hardly get him to stop talking about his school days.

The moral of the story? Be accessible to your children. Let them know you're there and available, but don't ask too many questions because that tends to make them clam up.

Keeping the Lines Open

Generally, communication between parents and children takes a nosedive right around the time the child enters fourth grade. After that, it gets better again for a couple of years, but goes downhill as soon as the child begins junior high school. Many parents are disappointed because they think they have great communication with their kids—"My son knows he can tell me anything"—and then all of a sudden it stops.

Your child will come in later than he's supposed to and you'll say, "Where have you been?"

"Nowhere."

"Well, what have you been doing?"

"Nothing."

"You mean you haven't been anywhere and you haven't been doing anything, and you're still an hour late getting home?"

The child will shrug and head for his bedroom.

Maybe you've already experienced this sort of behavior, and if you have, you know how hard it can be. But if your children have not yet reached this stage, let me tell you two very important things you need to know.

1. It's a perfectly natural part of the growth process, as long as your child does not go overboard with it—withdrawing into his room for hours at a time and having little or nothing to do with the rest of the family. As the child gets older, your role in his life is going to diminish, and the role of his peer group is going to grow greater. He'll be discussing his problems and fears, his likes and his dislikes, with his friends more than he will with his mom and dad. He will be helping to shape some of their attitudes about life and they will be doing the same to him. That's why it's *so* important that he have good, quality, moral friends.

2. The best thing you can do during this time is to let him know that you're always ready to listen, and that you are open to discuss anything that might be on his mind. (Notice I used the word "discuss." That implies a give-and-take conversation, and not a lecture.) Your child may not be anxious to talk to you right now, but it's important for him to know you're there and that you really care about what is on his mind. You may go through periods where communications aren't as strong as they once were, but if you keep the lines open, you'll never lose them altogether.

Two other key principles regarding family communications are:

• Realize the importance of mealtime as a catalyst for conversation. I suggest that, as often as possible, the entire family sit down together for dinner. I realize this can't always happen. Mom may have a meeting, or dad may have to work late. Ralphie may have a Little League game, or Ralphina may be involved in a youth activity at church. But there are bound to be at least two or three nights every week where the whole family can break bread together.

A friend of mine told me his 11-year-old daughter announced one night that theirs was the only family she knew that actually ate dinner together. This was a middle-child with a number of friends, so she wasn't talking about one or two other families in the neighborhood. More like 15 other middle class American families, and none of them ate together. That's tragic, because dinnertime provides the perfect opportunity for pleasant give-and-take conversation that includes and is respectful of every member of the family.

• Learn to listen to your child. Don't think you're the one who has to do all the speaking, or all the "teaching." Your child may have some insightful and imaginative ways of interpreting this marvelous world in which we live. Listen. You never know what you might learn!

Don't Make Comparisons

A surefire way to cause problems in the classroom and the family is to compare your children with others in the neighborhood or—even worse—with their brothers and sisters. First, let me mention other kids in the neighborhood.

Remember that old show, "Leave It To Beaver"? Well, one of the characters was a real brat named Eddie Haskell. He was forever getting Wally and The Beaver into trouble. Yet whenever Ward or June came around, he was the nicest, politest kid ever to be born onto this planet.

The amazing thing about the show—and the main reason you knew it was fiction—was that Mr. and Mrs. Cleaver saw right through Eddie Haskell. They *knew* the kid was a brat. But if this had been a real-life situation, Ward and June would have been more likely to tell their kids, "Why can't you be more like Eddie Haskell. He's such a nice boy!"

It's always amazed me that when parents pick out role models for their children, they tend to pick out the kids who are the biggest loudmouths, showoffs and cheats in school—but who are adept at "snowing" parents. That only adds to a child's resentment, as he thinks, "What? Mom wants me to be like *that* jerk?!"

Making comparisons between your own children is even worse. It promotes resentment and jealousy within the family and lowers the self-esteem of the child being told he doesn't measure up to his sibling's performance. You will do better if you always seek to communicate that you are interested in each child's honest effort to do *his best*, and that it's not as much the outcome as the effort that is important to you.

Here are three deadly ways to start sentences:

"Why can't you be more like..."

"Your brother (or sister) never would have..."

"You're the only one of our children who's ever..."

Why do I call these words "deadly"? Because they are sure to kill a child's self-image. In all of these instances, the child is being told, "You don't measure up;" "You're the worst child we have;" and so forth.

I recently visited with Jim, a man who had developed a resentment toward his slightly older brother while the two of them were growing up. His parents were always saying to him, "Why can't you be more like Jack?" Mom and dad were proud of Jack. Jack could do no wrong. Jim felt like he was living in the middle of the old Smothers Brothers routine, "Mom always liked you best," only this was real life.

Now they were in their mid-30's and had come back home for dad's funeral. It was the first time they had sat down and had a brother-to-brother talk in probably 20 years. In the course of the conversation, Jim told Jack how he had always resented the fact he had spent his entire childhood trying to measure up to the standards Jack had set.

When Jack heard that, his mouth fell open.

"What are you talking about?"

"Mom and dad were always asking me why I couldn't be more like you," Jim replied.

"You're kidding."

"No? Why?"

"Because they were always asking *me* why *I* couldn't be more like *you*?" Jack explained.

"Like *me*?"

"Yeah. You were better at making friends than I was. You were good in math, and I'd always been terrible at it. You were good at mechanical things, and I don't know a Phillips screwdriver from a flathead!"

By constantly comparing them to each other, the parents had driven a wedge between their two sons. The harm was deep and long-lasting.

It's amazing to see the damage well-meaning parents can inflict on their children when all they really mean to do is generate some motivation. Comparing a child with his brother or sister does not produce motivation. Rather it breeds anger and self-doubt.

Don't Keep Raising the Bar

Strive not to be the kind of parent who is "always raising the bar a little higher." In other words, some moms and dads treat their children like Olympic high-jumpers. As soon as the child shows he can jump over the bar, they raise it another notch or two. There is no time to appreciate the child's accomplishment, to allow him to bask in the glow of his success. Instead, the attitude is "Yes, I've seen you do that. Now let me see you do *this*!"

In our success-mad society, there are many books, cassette tapes, videotapes, etc., that tell us we always have to "shoot for the stars." We must always set high goals and work hard in order to achieve our greatest potential. There is truth to all of this, but it can be overdone. It can be harmful, especially when it comes to your child and his education.

One of the ways parents continually raise the bar on their children is by over-use of the word "should." This word implies to a child that he hasn't quite measured up to your expectations.

For example, try to stop yourself from making comments like:

"You should study every night, like your cousin Wendy."

"Come on. You should be able to do this."

"You should be reading at a higher level by now."

"You should be able to get an A in this course."

"You should be able to do as well as your sister. I checked with the counselor and she told me you're both in the same IQ range."

Here's another way of raising the bar. Suppose a child comes home with a report card that has three A's and a C. The parent who is always raising the bar would be the one to single out the C and say, "How come you didn't do better in this class?"

The child doesn't hear anything about the three A's. All he hears is, "You didn't do quite well enough. I'm raising the bar a little bit more."

We talked about this earlier when we discussed the problems brought about by parents who re-do what their children have already done. And before I'm through, I'm going to talk about it again. It is impossible to over-emphasize the danger of communicating to your child that he or she just doesn't measure up.

This can be done subtly, with just a tone of voice or arch of the eyebrow. Check yourself in these areas. Ask your spouse to check you as he or she watches you talk with the children. Are you conveying encouragement and support, or are you communicating disappointment and dissatisfaction? Always remember, you are your child's best teacher, not only when it comes to the academic side of life, but also when it comes to developing an overall attitude about himself and life in general.

I've seen children with tremendous I.Q.'s who seemed to fail at everything they tried. Why? Because the tendency to fail had been built into them. They *knew* they couldn't succeed, and so they didn't.

On the other side of the coin, I've watched kids who weren't particularly gifted go on to have outstanding academic careers. Again, the question is "Why?" Almost without exception, it was due to the loving, supportive attitudes of their moms and dads.

Time Consuming, But Worth It

In this chapter, we've discussed a few of the ways you can be your child's best teacher—how you can help him learn to read, write, and communicate verbally so he has the skills to be a success not only in school, but in life as well. Is it time consuming to do these things? You bet it is. Is it worthwhile? You will have to be the judge of that. How important are your children to you?

As for me, I know—because of my experiences as parent, teacher, and counselor—that depending on the schools to do the total job of teaching your child is like depending on a T-shirt for warmth when it's 30° below zero outside. It just doesn't work!

Exercises

• As soon as you can, set up an appointment with your children's teachers. Resolve to be involved in the educational process.

• Take your small child to the library. Get him a library card if he doesn't already have one. Help him pick out some books, and then set aside some time to read to him every day.

• Encourage your children's creativity by urging them to put on a play for you. You can make it a fun family project by fixing up some posters, making simple props, and making cookies or popcorn for the audience (and cast). You'll find that watching a "homemade" play is much more fun than a night of television—and much healthier for your family!

When Johnny and Jenny Go Off to School

A few years ago, there was a movie out called "Baby Boom." It starred Diane Keaton as a woman whose successful career was threatened by the birth of her son.

It wasn't all that terrific of a movie, and didn't stick around too long at local theaters, so you may not remember it. But there was one scene that gave me a chuckle—although I'll have to admit it was sort of painful humor.

In this scene, the mother takes her son to the park. He's not even walking yet; in fact, he's still drooling and chewing on his rattle. At the park she meets several other mothers, all with babies about her son's age, all of whom are already making plans to get their children into the best preschools in town. They are absolutely appalled when they find out Diane Keaton hasn't yet done anything about getting her child into one of these "name" schools. After all, there are long waiting lists. And, if she wants to get her son started on the right foot, she just *has* to get him a prestigious pre-school or kindergarten.

That particular scene gave me a chuckle because it was so absolutely absurd. But it hurt too, because it was so close to the truth.

Somewhere along the line, our society seems to have forgotten that children are children. We use them as status symbols, and we push them to grow up ahead of their time. Consequently, we're doing them, ourselves, and our society a grave disservice.

Whenever I read about some father who is teaching his 3-year-old daughter how to conjugate Latin verbs, or who has his still-in-diapers son solving complicated algebraic equations, I cringe inside. Such parents may produce geniuses— but I always wonder if those geniuses will live happy, productive lives, or grow up to be unhappy and neurotic.

Now I realize that occasionally a genius is born into this world—someone who is destined to be teaching at Harvard while all the other kids his age are in Miss Johnson's fifth-grade class. But too many parents today are determined to *turn* their kids into geniuses, and they're *pushing* much too hard in that direction.

Having said all that, let me emphasize that I am not at all opposed to getting a child into pre-school when he is 3 or 4 years old. This can be a worthwhile experience, very much to the good, but it must be kept in its proper perspective. Pre-school is not an adequate substitute for the things a child could learn at home. Nor is it designed to turn little Norbert into a latter-day Einstein.

Parents often ask me if I recommend that children go to pre-school. My answer is always that the experience can enrich a child's life and prepare him for the schooling that lies ahead, but it's certainly not necessary.

If there are few children in your neighborhood the same age as your pre-schooler, if he has no one to play with, then I strongly recommend pre-school. That's because I believe the emphasis in pre-school education should be on social learning and sharing, *not* academic experience.

While it's true that children at this age can learn a great deal about reading readiness and other academic interests, studies have shown that getting this head start does not guarantee they will do better in school later on. Again, if a child learns to interact well with other children and listen when the teacher reads to the class, then pre-school is a good experience.

Another reason pre-school can be healthy for a child is that it is good for him to get away from mom (or dad) two or three hours a day, two or three days per week. It begins to "wean" the child away from home so he will be comfortable and confident when it is time for him to enroll in school. Being away from home for any more than that amount of time, however, can be hard on the psyche of your average 3-year-old.

How to Choose a Pre-school

Another thing I'm often asked is how to choose a good pre-school. Well, the first thing to do is visit the school. See what the classrooms are like. Get a feeling for the day-to-day activities. If possible, spend some time at the school during the day, watching the teachers and children in action. I know this isn't always possible, but it is well worth the time invested. Here are a few of the things to look for during a visit:

1. *Balance between work and play.*

In my opinion, a good pre-school is one that has some structure, but not so much that it seems to be regimented and stifling. There should be a variety and rhythm in the activities. For example, a period of learning activities should be followed by a time of free play. I would want my child to profit from the experience, but as much as anything else, I would want him to have a good time and associate a learning environment with a fun environment.

2. *Liberal use of music.*

One thing I always look at when I'm considering a pre-school is its music program. Music is a great way for children to have fun and learn at the same time. Putting concepts like rules of math and grammar to music helps children retain them. Music is also an excellent means of teaching sentence development, vocabulary, listening skills, and so on.

Incidentally, this isn't just true for children. The Christian Broadcasting Network has developed a literacy program called *Sing, Spell, Read, and Write,* and it is apparently working very effectively not only with school-age children, but with adults as well. Music also helps develop imagination and creativity. It's important that children have the opportunity to act out songs and also make up their own.

3. *The neatness of the classroom.*

What I have to say about this may surprise you. That's because when I see a classroom that is too neat and tidy, I tend to scratch that school from my list. When a pre-school room has a pristine, spotless look, as if everyone there lives by the motto of "a place for everything and everything in its place," you can expect that the school is headed by an overly perfectionistic person. That is apt to create stress for the children. I don't want to see a classroom that is in complete disarray, over-run with crumpled up construction paper and crayons all over the floor, etc. I *do,* however, want to see a room that's just messy enough to let me know it's being used to its maximum benefit by an energetic group of pre-schoolers.

4. *Visual stimulation.*

Another thing I look for is a classroom that will give the child plenty of cheerful visual stimulation. I want to see colorful posters and collages, and I want the colors of the walls to be bright and cheerful. This isn't of primary importance, and I understand that some schools may be doing the best they can with what they have. Yet if I have to choose between a dull, neutral room and one that sparkles with life, you can bet that I'll choose the one that sparkles.

5. *Games and other creative activities.*

I also take a quick look around to see if there are plenty of materials and games to trigger the child's imagination. I look for toys and equipment that require action, and that will teach him something even as he's having a good time.

Are there messy, greasy fingerpaints? Great. A messy child is very often a learning child. If the school allows the child to work with clay, paste, and all sorts of other messy materials, that's terrific.

At this age, your child is still experiencing many things for the first time. Who knows what aptitude he may show? He may become the DaVinci of fingerpaints!

6. *Does it look like a "fun" place?*

Yes, I know the difference between a pre-school and an amusement park. I wouldn't want my children being taught every day by Chuck E. Cheese, but if there's anything *Sesame Street* has taught us, it's that learning doesn't have to be sterile and "academic." When our daughter Holly was 3, she attended an excellent pre-school, directed by a warm, affectionate leader and staffed by a responsive group of aids and teachers. Unfortunately, though, the school was controlled by a university. As bureaucracy would have it, a decision was handed down that it was time for a changing of the guard. The kind, caring director was replaced by a Ph.D. who decided to turn Holly's bright, cheerful pre-school into a "human learning laboratory."

It was quickly evident that Holly did not want to be part of any "human learning laboratory." She had been having a good time, and learning more than a few important things, with the school the way it was. It soon became a real hassle to get her to go to school each day.

Finally, one day she sat down on the sofa, folded both arms across her chest, and announced she simply wasn't going back. She was about to become a pre-school dropout!

I said, "All right, you can quit, but you have to call the director and tell her so yourself."

I didn't think she'd take me up on my bluff, but she wanted out so badly that she did exactly what I had asked. She marched to the phone, dialed the number, and lisped with all her 3-year-old dignity, "Thith ith Holly Leman, and I'm not coming to pre-school any more." And she didn't go back. Leave it to the first-born to take the bull by the horns! Holly was only one of many children in that school, and I'm sure there were many adversely affected by its transformation.

7. *Does the pre-school stress social development over academic development?*

We've already talked about the fact that children can be taught to read at an early age, and so I do believe a pre-school should put some emphasis on reading. Also, in today's computer age, it is important to give the child early training in numbers and math concepts. But, I also strongly believe a pre-school should stress social development over academic development, for at least two reasons.

• At this age, a child needs to learn: how to get along with others, that it's okay if he's away from mommy for awhile, and that it is possible for him to venture out from the safe, secure nest of his home.

• I have read several psychological studies that have concluded that academic training of children at the pre-school level does not make much difference during the elementary years. In other words, children who have not had pre-school education will do as well on standardized tests in the fourth, fifth, and sixth grade levels as children who had pre-school training that stressed academics.

Now I am not sure all the evidence is in, and later studies may reverse these findings. As far as we know right now, however, most of the benefits to be derived from the pre-school experience would seem to fit into the "social" category.

Now that we've discussed what to look for in a classroom, let's move on to an evaluation of the teaching staff.

1. Are the teachers outnumbered? It's vital that a pre-school have a good ratio of teachers to children. For example, in a class of 3-year-olds, a ratio of one teacher and one aid for every 16 children is ideal. If you find a ratio lower than that, it means your child is likely to get plenty of individual attention and that's great. However, if you see 22 children in a class with only one teacher and no aides, then you'd do well to keep looking.

2. Are the teachers suited to pre-schoolers? Do they seem to understand and know how to relate to them? In addition to checking the *qualifications* of the teachers in the school, I always notice *how they relate to the children* when they're talking to them. Does the teacher tower over the child, looking down at him like some fearsome giant, or does she get down on his level as often as possible? When a teacher bends or stoops down to meet the child at his or her level, it

indicates genuine interest. It demonstrates an awareness that the child is a person with individual needs and desires.

Of course, I don't expect teachers to go around the classroom on their hands and knees all day. But if I see a teacher who, at least occasionally, tries to get down on the child's level, I see someone who is thoughtful of the child's feelings. I like that.

3. Are the teachers well qualified? Don't be afraid to ask about the qualifications of the teachers with regard to background, training, and experience. You may be reluctant to ask some direct questions, especially if you're dealing with a church pre-school and the staff members are your friends and neighbors. Be that as it may, however, remember you are placing your child in the care of these people for significant periods of time. There's nothing wrong with wanting to make sure that your child is truly going to benefit from the situation.

What to Look for in a Christian School

Over the last 10 or 15 years, the Christian school movement has swept the country. There are hundreds of fine, Christ-centered schools that are as good academically, and in many instances even better, than the public schools in an area. Many Bible-believing parents, fed up with what they see as the failure of the public school system, have enrolled their children in Christian schools. On the other hand, there are many Christian parents who have opted to stick it out with the public schools, hoping to act as "salt and light." In essence, they have refused to abandon those schools to the "powers of darkness."

Parents often ask me whether I think they should send their children to Christian or public schools. My answer?

There is no clear-cut answer. It depends, for the most part, on the child and the quality of the schools under consideration.

I may be getting myself into hot water here, but the first thing I need to say is that just because a school bears the name "Christian" doesn't mean it's going to be a high quality school. Again, remember there are hundreds, perhaps even thousands, of excellent Christian schools. Yet there are some where the child will not get as good an education as in the public school. In that case, I would certainly opt for public school.

I don't know if you've ever seen a book called *The Christian Yellow Pages.* Many areas have one—a listing of businesses that are Christian-oriented or owned by Christians. I think it's a good idea for Christians to do business with other Christians wherever possible, so I'm not opposed to the concept. But, on the other hand, if I had an aching tooth, my first question about a dentist wouldn't necessarily be, "Is he a Christian?" I'd want to know, "Is he a good dentist?" I mean, if this person were incompetent I'd stay away—Christian or not!

That's the way I feel about Christian schools. When asked to choose between two schools and the only information I have is that one of them is public and one is Christian, I don't have enough information to make a good choice. After all, not all public schools are bad. Not all public school teachers are humanistic or atheistic. In fact, it's been my experience that there are many fine Christian teachers within public schools, doing their best to be a witness for Christ within the avenues open to them.

Furthermore, just because a school is advertised as "Christian" does not mean it is run in a Christ-like manner, or in a way conducive to children's growth and learning—spiritually, mentally, emotionally, socially, and physically.

Finding a good Christian school is like finding a good preschool. Parents are wise to take a look at any school—to determine its philosophy of teaching and see how it implements that philosophy.

Also, I caution parents that the Christian school is not a magic answer or panacea for every problem. For example, if your child is having major disciplinary problems in a public school, there's no reason to think he's going to do great in a Christian atmosphere. Yes, in some instances the change will help, but not always.

There are currently more than three million students enrolled in Christian schools throughout the United States, and that delights me. These schools provide a welcome and often necessary alternative to what the public schools are doing. They are not perfect, however, and any parent who expects perfection will wind up disappointed.

What would I look for in a Christian school?

• How long has the school been in existence, and what is its track record? How long has the current administrator or principal been there? What about the teachers? Just because the school has experienced personnel doesn't guarantee it's a quality institution, but a high rate of turnover could be a sign of problems.

• What is the basic purpose of the school, and how is it reflected in the Scriptures? Along with this, I think it's important to look for a school that stresses a positive attitude and majors on the "dos" of the Christian life, instead of one that comes across as authoritarian and focuses on the "don'ts."

• Does the school have programs to deal with "special" children, those with learning disabilities or those who are gifted? Does it have the ability to meet unique problems and circumstances that may arise in dealing with students?

• Does the school use curriculum developed by a consensus of its teaching staff, or does it strictly adhere to curriculum bought from a publisher? A packaged curriculum can be a good starting place, but it must be modified and tailored to the needs of the children.

• What are the qualifications of the teachers? What are their experiences? Do they have all the necessary credentials?

• Finally, I wouldn't enroll my child in a Christian school that did not have a good program in athletics and fine arts. Due to tax uprisings across the country, many public schools have had to cut back in these areas. However, I don't believe these are "fringe benefits." They are important to the overall education and development of the child. For many children, particularly in certain grades or periods of their educational careers, participation in sports or the school band can be the most important part of school life. For many a child, his "real thing" is playing the clarinet, marching in the band, or learning how to be part of a team.

Earmarks of a Good Teacher

Remembering that the relationship between any school and the home is critical, and that you are the most important teacher your child will ever have, I do think there are some definite ways to tell if your child's teachers are doing a good job. Cliff Schimmels, an associate professor in the education department of Wheaton College who has spent several years teaching and coaching in public high schools, wrote an excellent book called *How to Help Your Child Survive and Thrive in Public School*. In it, he outlines several ways parents can distinguish between good and bad teaching in any school, public or private.[1] He says that a teacher's violation of one or two of these points does not necessarily mean he's not fit to teach—but that it may indicate you need to take a closer look at the situation.

1. *Good teachers read and return homework assignments.*

Are your children conscientious about their homework or do they say things like, "Oh, it doesn't matter. He never reads it anyway." If a teacher gives out homework assignments but then never seems to check or give them back, it's time to wonder if he is really interested in seeing his students learn the subject matter, or if he's just giving out busywork. How students do on their homework is an excellent gauge of whether they are grasping the concepts being taught. It can show teachers where a particular area needs reinforcement, or where certain students need special help.

Incidentally, while we're on the subject of homework, let me tell you that I make it a point to never ask my children whether they have homework, or how much homework they have. That is *their* responsibility, not mine. If they want my help with a particular subject they can come and ask me for it. If a child won't do his homework unless mom and dad constantly push him to, then he's not learning personal responsibility.

2. *Good teachers give worthwhile assignments.*

Schimmels gives the example of a teacher who asked her students to copy 96 long sentences from a textbook, and then punctuate them properly. Her objective was to teach her students how to use commas. He asks why she didn't give the

---

1. Cliff Schimmels, *How to Help Your Child Survive and Thrive in Public School,* (Old Tappan, NJ: Fleming H. Revell, 1979).

students a print-out of those sentences, and just ask them to add the commas. That would have been much easier for them, and it would have done just as good a job of teaching.

Ask your children about their homework assignments, just so you know the sorts of things they're doing every night. If you see something that seems out of line or doesn't make sense, talk to the teacher about it.

3. *Good teachers stay in the classroom.*

Did you ever have one of those teachers who would give you an assignment, and then leave the room for 15 or 20 minutes? What happened when he left? If your school was typical, kids started shooting rubber bands, throwing spit-wads, whacking each other with erasers, and generally giving every indication that man indeed descended from the apes! A good teacher may have to leave the classroom on occasion, but he or she will also want to make sure time in the class is used wisely. That means staying in the room as much as possible.

4. *Good teachers are organized.*

They know where they're going, and should impart that knowledge to your child. What are we going to learn in this class? How are we going to learn it? What special projects and other events will be a part of the classwork?

A companion to organization is preparation. Schimmels notes that a teacher who stays up late at night preparing an interesting dynamic lesson plan is going to be much more effective in the classroom than a teacher who hasn't changed one approach or one note in several years.

In the mid-'70s, I heard about a high school science teacher who, while plodding dully through his notes in a classroom lecture, said, "and this is why man will never be able to land on the moon." He needed to update his notes *and* his approach to science!

5. *Good teachers communicate with parents.*

If your child isn't doing well in a particular class, the teacher needs to let you know about it. If there's something you can do to improve his performance, you need to know about that, too. As a parent, it is your responsibility to make sure your child's teacher knows you are interested and available. A good teacher, however, remembers that communication is a two-way street, and will not necessarily wait for you to come to him.

6. *Good teachers don't lose control of themselves.*

Let's admit the fact that teaching is a difficult profession. Going face to face with 25 or more energetic children every day is not easy. But even though that is true, and even though the teacher must retain control of the classroom, there is no call for a teacher to ridicule a student, strike out in anger, or resort to violence. Any teacher who does so needs to go on a nice long holiday.

7. *Good teachers give students a sense that the material is important.*

"Why should I learn this? I'm never going to use it."

"I can't learn this stuff. It's *soooo* boring!"

Have you ever heard comments like these? You may still hear them even if your child has an excellent teacher, but chances are you won't hear them very often. A good teacher instills a sense of excitement about the subject he teaches, to get his students to understand why they need to have a proper understanding of it.

These seven points are all important to consider when evaluating your child's teachers. For the Christian school, however, I would add one more: A good teacher can be measured by how he or she communicates the faith. The Christian teacher should have a blend of biblical authority and integrity, mixed with a positive view of life and people.

It All Comes Back to You

After all we've said in the last couple chapters, it all comes back to the fact that you are, indeed, the most important teacher your child will ever have. You can be the most effective by far. Because you have that role in your child's life, there is also much you can do to support your child's schools and teachers.

Let those teachers know you care. Communicate your interest in supporting them. If you appreciate the job they are doing, let them know. It doesn't take much effort to send a card and say, "You're doing a terrific job!" Yet that is the kind of encouragement that will help to turn a good teacher into a great one.

A few final thoughts before we move on:

• As you work with the child's school and teachers, be sure you always center on what will benefit the child. Some parents make it their personal business to keep the schools and teachers in line. They get so caught up in the political nature of the struggle that they lose sight of what's really important—the children. Whatever you do, it should always be done with one aim in mind: helping your child become the best person he can possibly become.

• Keep in mind that each of your children is unique. Each has his own particular interests, needs, weaknesses, and strengths. You cannot treat them all alike, nor expect them all to handle the business of school in the same way.

• Always take time to communicate with your child. Listen to him. Discipline consistently with gentleness and with love. Take time to show interest in what he's doing, even if it means you have to give up some "fun" activity or change your schedule in some other way.

• Always listen to your child's feelings. Remember, if he talks with you about the little things when he's small, he will be much more likely to talk with you about the bigger things when he gets older, and his problems become more complex.

• Keep in mind that education is a long-term process. There will be many ups and downs for your child during his years on the educational merry-go-round. Be sure you are always along for the ride!

6

Your Child's Personality

*D*onna was having serious problems with her 12-year-old son, Jason. He was getting terrible grades in school, she had found a pornographic magazine under his bed, and she had caught him more than once climbing in through his bedroom window well after the time he was supposed to be in bed asleep. On those occasions, he wouldn't say anything more about where he had been except that he had been "out." She was also worried because she had reason to believe he had started smoking. If he was doing all these things at this age, she had good reason to wonder what he'd be doing by the time he was 15 or 16.

Jason was a middle child, a very sociable boy, as many middle-borns are. He seemed particularly susceptible to peer pressure, and Donna said she was always fighting the impulse to say things like "If everybody else jumped off the Empire State Building, would you do that, too?" As I talked to her about Jason's personality, it became apparent he had always had a stubborn, rebellious streak.

"When he was just 5 or 6 years old and I'd ask him to scoot his chair down at the dinner table to give his brother more room, he'd always say, 'Why can't *he* scoot down?'

"If I asked him to pick up his jacket because he'd left it lying on the floor, he'd say something like, 'Justin left *his* jacket on the floor yesterday, and you didn't say anything to *him!*' "

In other words, Jason had always been your typical strong-willed child. As we looked back together, Donna and I began to see ways Jason had been encouraged in his behavior. Instead of standing strong and making the boy do exactly what he was told to do, Donna and her husband very often backed down. Every little thing they asked him to do became a battle, and they decided very early on it simply wasn't worth it. To avoid confrontation and aggravation, they gave in to him far too often.

Thus encouraged, Jason had become more and more insistent he would only do what *he* wanted to do. Of course, even though he was very rebellious where mom and dad were concerned, his behavior was still dictated by the styles and attitudes of his peer group, to the point where he was definitely headed for trouble.

Fortunately, Donna and her husband realized things had to change where Jason was concerned. They resolved to stiffen their defenses and stand up to him, and they did. Their newfound resolve, along with some healthy doses of Reality Discipline (see Chapter 2), eventually helped alter their son's behavior. But it wasn't easy. In fact, they had a pretty rough time of it with him for a couple of years, and there are still occasional flareups with Jason, who is now 17. (Show me a parent who doesn't have an occasional flareup with his teenager, and I'll show you someone who just stepped out of a 1950's sitcom!)

It's not my purpose here to talk about what these parents did to bring Jason's behavior into line with their expectations. Rather, Jason's story is an indicator of something I've seen over and over again. Namely, that a child's personality is shaped very early in his life. The old Proverb says, "As the twig is bent, so grows the tree," and that's pretty much the truth. The decisions you make, very early in your child's life, help to mold and shape him into the sort of adult he will become. When I think about a person's personality being shaped in early childhood, I always remember Elaine.

She was 32, the mother of a 7-year-old son and a 4-year-old daughter, and she had been married and divorced three times. Elaine's first husband, Bill, had been a real rat. He was unfaithful, and lied to her constantly. He was a problem drinker who didn't seem to have the slightest bit of ambition, and could not hold a job. He seemed quite content to let Elaine, an elementary schoolteacher, support him.

After four years of putting up with his cheating, drinking, and failure to work, she filed for divorce, even though it meant she would be a single mother to her baby boy. She had been single for less than a year when she fell in love with Gus. He looked like just what she needed. He would care for her and be a good provider. He wasn't anything like her first husband. Until they got married.

Then the *real* Gus appeared. He, too, was a problem drinker who wouldn't keep his hands off other women. He had a steady job, but was always on the verge of losing it because of his alcoholism. Elaine stayed with him a few years, during which her little girl was born, but finally decided she had had enough. She again filed for divorce.

105

Third time's a charm? Not in this case. The next guy she fell in love with was a fellow named Dale. He made her other two husbands look like magna cum laude graduates of the Dale Carnegie self-improvement course. He not only had the qualities of her first two husbands, but he was violent as well. He would often slap her around and threaten to harm the children. She was smart enough to know that no woman should put up with that sort of abuse. Once again, she found herself walking the single side of the street, wondering what was wrong with her that made her pick three losers in a row.

At that point, she knew there must be something more than bad luck involved. She came to see if I could help her understand, and hopefully change, whatever it was in her personality that attracted her to such men. I told her that a lifestyle analysis was necessary if I was going to provide her with the answers. This involves a series of questions regarding the person's family—mother, father, siblings, and the interrelationships within the family. We talked about the kind of atmosphere present in the home when Elaine was a little girl, as well as her recollections of early childhood. Finally, we examined all of the male-female relationships Elaine had experienced.

It was easy to determine that Elaine's mother had been the dominant figure in her life. In fact, she was the dominant person in the family, and ruled the roost with an iron hand. A teacher by profession, she hadn't taught since the first two years in her marriage. Elaine's father was a successful businessman who provided well for the family, and Elaine's mother had not needed to work. Instead, she had involved herself in community affairs such as drives for the Heart Fund, PTA activities, and church work. Elaine told me that she knew, from a very young age, that she was supposed to marry a doctor, a lawyer, a banker, or someone else who could be looked up to—someone who had status and the capability of making a large amount of money.

She was the youngest of three sisters, and had been the "black sheep" of the family. In other words, she was the one who rejected the family values and goals.

Older sister Martha had married a prominent attorney—just the type of man mom would have picked for her. Judy had married a banker who lived in the same town as her mom and dad.

Meanwhile, Elaine was the one who always seemed to be at odds with her mother. She remembered, for example, how her mother had always wanted to dress her daughters in feminine, lacy dresses—to have them look like little dolls. Elaine didn't want anything to do with that. She preferred pants, and was not at all shy about letting her mother know how she felt.

As we talked, she recalled the countless hassles she and mom had gotten into over the way she wanted to dress, the boys she wanted to date, whether or not she could see certain movies, wear lipstick, or...well, you can just about name it and Elaine and her mother had gone round and round about it.

Why had Elaine seemed to go out of her way to make life rough for her mother? She really didn't know. During the process of the lifestyle analysis, however, Elaine began to see there were some logical reasons for her behavior. She realized, for instance, that Martha had been "Little Miss Perfect." She would have been a tough act for Mother Teresa to follow. She was a member of the National Honor Society and captain of the cheerleading squad. She was also a member of the school yearbook staff and involved in a number of activities in the church. Everyone who knew Martha seemed to think the world of her.

As far as Judy was concerned, she was an excellent athlete, and had a pretty good singing voice. She wasn't a straight-A student like Martha, and seemed content with her usual assortment of B's. There were usually a goodly number of A's sprinkled into the mix, too.

Between the two of them, Elaine's two sisters had pretty much cornered the market on "wonderful things to be." They had a lock on academics, creativity, athletics, music, and leadership. About the only role left open for Elaine was the one she had taken: black sheep of the family.

This was the way she could establish her own individuality, to tell all the world—especially her mother and sisters—that she was her own person. She didn't have to be what anyone else expected her to be. Unfortunately, Elaine's behavior had hurt her more than anyone else. When I pointed out that one of the ways she got back at her mother was to marry men like Bill, Gus, and Dale, her eyes flew open in painful recognition.

No, she hadn't consciously set out to hurt her mother. She hadn't said, "This guy looks like a real loser, so I'll marry him to show mom up." Yet underneath it all, deep down on the subconscious level, that's exactly what she had done.

What's more, her marriage decisions reflected her self-image. She thought she was no good, not worth loving. After all, she sure couldn't measure up the success of her two sisters. She picked men who would treat her the way she thought she deserved to be treated, and that was not good at all.

I recall Elaine sitting in her office one afternoon, sobbing as she told me of all the times as a teenager she had slept with young men. These were boys who didn't really care about her, and she knew that. She let them use her because she grew up thinking she deserved to be used.

I asked her if she had ever experienced sexual satisfaction with *any* male, including her three husbands. She shook her head. I told her that this was further evidence that she didn't see herself as worthy of having the opportunity to experience sexual fulfillment. She told me she was disgusted with herself, and sick of feeling like a "sexual receptacle."

How Elaine Turned It Around

It was at about this point that Elaine began to take some steps to turn her life around. The first thing she had to do— and it wasn't going to be easy—was share her feelings with her mother. Elaine told me she hadn't really talked with her mother for 12 years, and it would be very difficult now, because she felt she would have to eat a healthy helping of humble pie.

Actually, it didn't really work out that way, because mom was happy to know Elaine was willing to sit down and talk. She didn't like the way things were between them. She was just as anxious as her daughter to get it all straightened out.

After they had met, Elaine told me they had talked for an entire afternoon and evening and on into the wee hours of the morning sharing about her life, and especially her childhood. She told her mother she felt the same way now that she had felt when she was a little girl no older than 5 or 6.

She explained that she felt inadequate when it came to measuring up to mom's standards, or in trying to compete with the accomplishments of her sisters. She said she had always felt as if she were in competition with the other girls, but that the competition was hopeless because they were so much better than she was, in so many ways.

Elaine also recognized that one of the problems in her life was that she had never had a loving and supportive father.

While he was a whiz when it came to business, her father didn't seem to care much whether he spent any time with his children. He hadn't been the kind of dad who was willing to get down on the floor to play games with them, or share his time with them on an individual or group basis. Elaine even told her mom about her recent discovery—that reaching out for male attention in her teenage years was a way to try to find the love she so desperately wanted from her father.

Now, don't think a light came on in Elaine's mind, and then it was all easy from there. Her childhood had left many deep wounds on her personality—wounds which had never received proper treatment, and had not healed as they should have. In some instances, this meant going back and re-opening those wounds so they could be dealt with properly, and the pain dispensed with once and for all.

It was a painful process, yes, but absolutely necessary. Because she knew that, Elaine was willing to go through it.

Fortunately, Elaine's case has a happy ending. Several years later she married for the fourth time, to a man who loved and respected himself enough that he was able to treat Elaine with the love and respect she deserved. Rob was a widower at the age of 39, and was just the right husband for her. Several months after they married, Elaine and I talked again. She was quick to tell me that she never knew a sexual life could be so fulfilling and rewarding. For the first time in her life, she was really able to communicate on an intimate level with a man, to give herself in a deeply loving way, and to receive the same from him.

The "I Only Count When" Game

Do you see how Elaine's early experiences in life, her perceptions of herself, and her family came together to form her lifestyle? One of the things Elaine had done was play a little game I call "I Only Count When." In her situation, it was "I only count when I'm noticed," and so she sought attention, especially from men and boys, however she could get it.

I want to warn you, as a parent, not to play the "I Only Count When" game with your child. He or she needs to understand and feel deep down that he counts, not because of anything he does or is, but just because he's your child. Make sure he knows you love him very much, *pure* and *simple*. Be careful not to treat him in a way that makes him believe any of the following:

"I only count when I'm noticed."

"I only count when I'm good."

"I only count when I'm successful."

"I only count when I look good."

"I only count when I have a boyfriend (or girl-friend)."

"I only count when I'm the center of attention."

"I only count when I have plenty of money."

I could go on and on with the list, but I'm sure you understand what I'm saying. We hear often that a person's personality is formed in the first few years of his life. I'm here to tell you that it is absolutely true. Early experiences are very, very important.

Attention-Getting Behavior (and Worse)

Before we conclude our discussion regarding a child's developing personality, I need to spend a few moments talking about three annoying and potentially destructive types of behavior. They are:

1. Attention-getting.
2. Attention-demanding.
3. Revengeful.

One of the common behaviors we see in children is attention-getting behavior. Children have the need to belong to the family. If a child fails to find his place within the home, he will undoubtedly try to find it elsewhere. Elsewhere might mean drugs, promiscuity, failure in school, or anything else.

Attention-getting behavior, however, does not always manifest itself in negative ways. The child who strives to get straight A's in school may also be demonstrating attention-getting behavior. He has simply chosen to get that attention from his parents, teachers, and peers through his school-work. There are all kinds of payoffs and reinforcements for such children—everything from stars and happy faces at the top of a paper to A's on report cards and hugs from mom or dad. The child who is "Mother's Little Helper," may also be demonstrating attention-getting behavior, as may the little one who wants to help his daddy rake leaves or cut the grass.

It is important for a child to find *positive* ways he can receive reinforcement, very early in life. If a child does not get attention in a positive fashion, you can bet he's going to go after it in a negative way. And you don't have to let your mind wander very far to determine how many different ways a child can get attention in a negative sense. There's bedwetting, whining, crying, lying, stealing, interrupting, and being the world's biggest goof-off in school. Those are just for starters! Again, if a child fails to get attention in a positive sense, he will move to negative behaviors in order to gain attention and notoriety.

Even though it's admirable for a child to want to help his parents or get straight A's in school, here again, the thing to watch out for is the "I Only Count When I'm Noticed" game.

While your child needs to understand that doing his best in school or helping mommy is wonderful, you have to be careful not to convey that you love him *only* because he's a big helper, or because he does well in school, or for any reason that ties his self-worth to performance.

When a Child Demands Attention

Occasionally, a child will move beyond mere attention-getting behavior into the realm of attention-*demanding* behavior. This is the child who says, "I'm going to make you pay attention to me no matter what."

He may hold his breath until he starts to turn blue. He may stamp his feet and kick and scream until the neighbors come over and ask you to, "Please, give that child what he wants!"

Or he may take a crayon and decorate one of the walls at home with his favorite swear words. (Unfortunately, any child who's been to a movie rated anything worse than "G" knows plenty of swear words. They probably won't be spelled exactly right, but you'll certainly be able to catch the meaning.)

Of course, just about every child who has ever existed has lapsed into attention-demanding behavior at one time or another. Children are like adults in that they sometimes get cranky, irritable, or feel that nobody is paying attention to them. Most of the children I see in my private practice however, are those who demonstrate attention-demanding behavior on a steady basis. They don't seem to know how to relate to their parents, or the world at-large, in anything but a brattish, obnoxious fashion. They are saying, "I'm going to be so obnoxious that you're not going to ignore me." Every once in awhile, when one of them leaves my office, I breathe a little prayer, "Thank you Lord, that he isn't *my* child!" Yes, attention-demanding behavior can be overcome, but it's very hard to put up with in the meantime.

Occasionally, a worried parent will ask me why his or her child behaves in this fashion. "I don't know what he wants. He'll throw a tantrum over the most insignificant thing."

The answer is that he's doing it purely and simply because he's figured out it's the best way to get his parents' attention. It gives him power over his parents. For this reason, the attention-demanding child may also be said to be "power-driven."

How do you know if your child is demonstrating attention-demanding behavior? Pay attention to your own emotions, and you'll know. If your child is acting in a way that makes you annoyed or slightly upset, you're probably dealing with an attention-getting child. If your admonition to the child makes him temporarily stop behaving in the aggravating way, you're probably dealing with an attention-getting child. If, however, your admonition merely intensifies the misbehavior or action, then you're probably coping with an attention-demanding, power-driven child. And, if your child's behavior is so troubling that you feel like punching him in the nose, then you're dealing with a power-driven, attention-demanding child—one who is doing everything he can to put himself in charge.

The Revengeful Child

In a moment, I'm going to give you some practical advice for dealing with attention-getting or attention-demanding behavior. Before I do, I want to tell you about the third level. That is, the child who exhibits revengeful behavior.

Most juvenile delinquents and gang members are into revenge-type behavior. Their goal isn't just to annoy or irritate, but to hurt.

The child's perception is, "I've been hurt by life, or by my parents, so I have the right to strike back." If you end up feeling hurt by a misbehaving child, you can assume the child is into revengeful behavior. If you find yourself asking, "How could he do this to me?" then you're probably dealing with revenge. Unfortunately, revengeful behavior is not easy to deal with, nor is it easy to correct. It usually stems from deep-seated anger and disappointment. If you have a child demonstrating revengeful behavior, the best thing you can do is seek treatment from a competent therapist.

One of the great tragedies of revengeful behavior is that it often manifests itself in teenage suicide. The young person who wants to take revenge on his parents thinks, "I know what I'll do. I'll kill myself. That will show them." And that's exactly what he does. No, he hasn't thought it through to the point where he realizes the severity of what he's contemplating. He just wants revenge. He'll go to any length to get it.

So, there you have three troubling behaviors children may manifest early in their lives: attention-getting, attention-demanding, and revengeful. If you don't work to eliminate those behaviors as soon as you see them, you could be headed for major trouble later on.

And remember, parents don't have to give in every time to reinforce these concepts; they just have to give in every once in a while. Reinforcement on an intermittent scale will keep children misbehaving. The message is clear: Misbehave, cry, or fuss and ol' mom or dad will give in. What a great way to teach irresponsibility!

How do you deal with these types of behavior? First, some basic rules for all three.

1. You can tell the child straight out, "It seems like you really need attention. If that's what you want, why don't you come over here and let me give you a hug or a kiss. You don't

have to act that way." Or you can simply reassure the child that mom and dad will always have enough hugs and kisses for all the children in the family, and there isn't any need to compete for attention or affection.

2. If you ignore a particular behavior of an attention-getting child, you can usually get the behavior to stop.

3. Avoid reminding and coaxing the attention-getting child. This is not easy to do. It's much easier to call the attention-getter three times to the dinner table. That's what he wants you to do because it makes you pay special attention to him. Call the child to the table once. If he doesn't come, don't call again. Instead, sit down and eat the meal without him. Let the child experience hunger as the result of his choice. And then, do yourself a favor. Don't feel badly about the poor tyke having to go to bed with an empty stomach. It's a small price to pay for the valuable lesson he is learning.

Whatever the area of misbehavior, do not give in to it. Then, just as important, do not give in to guilt later on because you feel like "an old meany." You're not being mean. You're building character into your child's life, and that's more important than his temporary discomfort or anger.

4. Maximize actions and minimize words. When I ask children how many times a parent has to call them for dinner, they usually tell me three times. Then they go on to tell me that the first time is designed just to get their attention, the second time communicates that mom (or dad) is beginning to become angry, and the third time (always spoken in a sharp, direct manner) means, "Hey, I mean it. You get in here right now!" We need to stop playing these kinds of games. They are senseless and they teach irresponsibility. They let your children know they don't have to pay attention to you until your voice goes up an octave or two, and the veins in your neck begin to bulge. The Bible says to, "let your yes be

yes and your no be no," because anything more than that comes from the devil. Leman's paraphrase of that says, "let your yes mean yes, your no mean no, and your come to the table mean come to the table—otherwise you're going to have a devil of a time!"

5. Look for times in a child's life when you can give attention by means of encouragement—pleasant, happy times, when things are going well.

When you are dealing with a power-driven child, you must resist the temptation to challenge the child. A parent's first reaction is usually, "I'm going to *make* him do it," and that's understandable. Yet all that does is get you involved in a struggle of wills, and that's *not* what you want. You want to stay above that, and on an even keel emotionally. If the child doesn't come to the table when you call him, then he misses his dinner. If he has been told to pick up his toys or he can't watch television, and he refuses to pick up his toys, then the television goes off. There's no other way around it. Once you have established what the consequence will be for a certain behavior or lack of behavior, you have to follow through. Be as cool, calm, and collected as you can be. Do your best to avoid becoming angry. But, don't remove the consequence.

Sometimes, the power-driven child just has to be given a chance to make his own choices, even if those choices are wrong. For example, a child who chooses to throw a temper tantrum has a right to do so, as long as he throws it somewhere out of your sight so you don't have to see him. It would be most appropriate, for instance, to pick up the child without saying a word and put him just outside the door, locking the door behind him if necessary. Tell him that when he's through with his tantrum he should let you know so you can let him back into the house. You can be sure the tantrum will dissolve in a matter of minutes. It's absolutely no fun to misbehave when there's nobody there to watch.

With the revengeful child you are apt to want to say, "Okay, if you want to war with me, I can war with you," or, "If you want to play a power game, I can be powerful, too." However, the best strategy is to try to be reasonable and offer a chance for the establishment of mutual respect. Showing your child you're willing to listen and discuss the situation in an atmosphere of respect can go a long way toward defusing revengeful behavior.

I strongly suggest parents avoid retaliation when revengeful behavior occurs. Fight the temptation to say, "I feel hurt by all this." As painful as it may be for you to face, that's exactly what the child wants. If you admit that his behavior has hurt you, you're giving him the payoff he's after, and you're just about ensuring it will continue. Communication is the key to turning around this behavior, and it often takes a great deal of communication to put the pieces back together.

Other Challenging Behaviors

Let me tell you briefly about some of the other behaviors and lifestyles we see developing in very young children:

1. *The shy child.*

I have yet to meet a shy child who is not a very powerful person. Children often use their shyness as a way of making people pay attention to them. I remember a little girl I worked with several years ago who spoke in such a soft voice that it was almost impossible to understand her. It was several minutes before I realized what she was doing. As our conversation continued, I found myself leaning toward her to such an extent that I had almost fallen out of my chair. She was being mighty powerful with me.

2. *The controller.*

This is the child who states through his behavior that he has to be the one in control of everything. If he's not the first, the best, the winner, the boss, then he's not happy. This is the child who will shut off the video game when he sees he's going to lose, or who will overturn the board game for the same reason. The key here is not to give in and let the child win all the time, but to make sure he understands consequences will be forthcoming if he persists in his behavior. Then, stick to your guns. Again, never discipline a child in anger or to take revenge for the fact that he has disappointed you, but because you are interested in his personal development.

3. *The martyr.*

Occasionally this lifestyle may be seen even in young children. This is the child who doesn't think he's good enough, who has to give to everybody, but can't allow anybody to give back to him. He or she obviously needs to be encouraged to see himself as a worthy and worthwhile person.

4. *The achiever.*

The achiever is the child who has to be perfect and do everything that is expected of him. He wants to bring home all A's, and will be devastated by a single B, or perhaps even an A-minus. This child needs to see that your love and appreciation for him are not tied to his performance.

It's important for parents to see that these life themes are just *expressions of the child trying to find his place in the family.*

The Time for Decisive Action

I've mentioned before that children often choose their "misbehaving places" very carefully. They love to act up in a store or in a restaurant, or someplace else where they feel you can't do very much about it. They understand the power they hold over you in such circumstances.

Another situation in which children are prone to act up is when you are visiting in the home of a friend or acquaintance. They know they've got you on the spot there. You may start off with a threat, but you'll wind up offering just about anything if only they'll stop embarrassing you!

Church is another favorite spot for children to misbehave. Have you ever seen a parent in the choir try to be discreet as he makes faces, coughs, and makes *subtle* threatening gestures to a misbehaving child sitting in the auditorium? He looks strange singing "Amazing Grace," with that angry glare on his face, but until church is over and he can get the child home, there's not much else he can do. For the time being, the child has the poor choir member at his mercy, and he knows it.

I'll never forget the time I was called into a Sunday school class to consult with a group of sixth-graders who were giving a young male teacher a great deal of grief. We talked about the need for individual responsibility in a group setting, and discussed some of the things that might be done to deal with misbehavior in the classroom. One of the suggestions I made was that if a sixth-grader was not big enough to remain in the group in a responsible manner, the teacher needs to take the child to his parent. One of the power-driven children smirked and smugly told me this could never work with him.

I asked him why not and he said, "Well, my mom is the organist."

I replied that I didn't see any problem with that.

"Well, my mom is in the church service when we're in Sunday school, so I couldn't possibly go where she is, because she's in front of the whole church."

I responded once again, "Gary, I still don't see the problem." The boy's expression began to change as it dawned on him that I meant what I was saying. If a child was misbehaving he should be taken directly to his parent, no matter what the parent might be doing at the time. I could see the terror creeping across the boy's face that he was envisioning what it would be like to be marched up to the front of the auditorium and, as the eyes of the congregation were upon him, be plunked down beside his mother.

When he told me his mom would get really mad, I answered, "Gary, you're probably right. I think she's going to get very mad, but I'm sure you can handle it." That ended our conversation, and I might add that it ended the problem of Gary misbehaving in class.

What had I done? Nothing more than tell the boy he was going to be responsible for his actions. If he persisted in misbehaving, he would have to accept the punishment prescribed for the occasion—even if that meant embarrassing him in front of the entire church, and making his mother "really mad."

We had said, in essence, "You've got the choice. You can behave in the classroom, or we can take you to your mom, who is legally responsible for your behavior." Regardless of the social situation, and regardless of the embarrassment it may cause, this is the kind of discipline that really works and that has a lasting effect on children.

A Watched Late Bloomer Never Blooms

If you've got a "late bloomer" in your home and you've been scratching your head nightly, looking at the ceiling and wondering when this kid is going to turn things around, let me give you the answer. He'll probably turn it around the day his parents make the decision to *stop doing for him,* and instead *place the responsibility squarely on his shoulders,* where it belongs. Only then can he take charge of his life.

Academically, there are basically two ways attention-seeking children can get the attention they crave. The first is overachieving; the second is underachieving. Many parents pay off the second type of behavior by running to the child's school, checking with the counselor, double-checking with the teacher, and then taking the nonachiever to counselors and psychologists of different varieties for explanations as to why the child is not achieving. Not achieving my eye! He's achieved what he wanted to achieve—getting mom and dad involved in his life in a really big way.

The only way we parents can provide motivation for the nonachiever or late bloomer is to step out of his academic life completely, and let him become accountable for his education. And parents, if you feel your child's behavior in school is a reflection on you and you communicate this to him, you're really asking for it. Kids can use their nonachievement as a real thorn in their parents' side. It's a beautiful way of keeping mom and dad over the proverbial barrel.

Some time ago, I worked with the parents of 13-year-old Freddie. He had just been thrown out of school for the fourth time during the seventh-grade year. School policy stated that in order for Freddie to get back into school, mom and dad would have to come and meet with the principal.

When the time came, mom and dad made it clear they would not do that. They told Freddie his education was over, and that they had no intention of enrolling him again.

Freddie didn't mind staying home—at first—but it got old real quick. He was terribly bored. He missed his friends.

He missed being the center of attention in the classroom. He was discovering how much school meant to him, in several different ways.

When the new school year rolled around, Freddie's mom and dad gave in to his pleas and allowed him to attend another school. But prior to the start of classes, they sat down with him and told him their expectations, with regard to both his behavior and his academic progress. They told him that he had to have a C average or better in order to be involved in anything extracurricular, including football, which was one of his true passions. Furthermore, he would not be allowed to go out on school nights unless it was a very special occasion.

And, because Freddie had been spending his allowance on things they did not approve of—like cigarettes and marijuana—they weren't going to give him one anymore. They told him if he wanted to do something like mow a few lawns around the neighborhood to make some money, it would be his choice as to how to spend it. Their hope was that having to work hard to earn his own money would make him less inclined to throw it away.

Freddie's parents essentially gave him the chance to start all over again. Because he was in a new school, he wasn't expected to behave in a certain way. He was free to rebuild his reputation into something a bit more positive than before—which is exactly what he did. He studied hard, made good grades, and was no longer a discipline problem. The boy had learned school was a privilege, not a right, and that he could no longer use his parents in his usual high-handed manner.

When I tell this story, someone always asks what would have happened if Freddie didn't change. Or, what if he liked staying at home and not doing much of anything every day? Well, first of all, that wasn't really very likely. Almost always, as soon as parents make children responsible for their own actions, a change in behavior and attitude takes place. Now and then, I will come across a situation where the child was incorrigible. He didn't care what his parents did, he wasn't going to change.

So if you've done everything you can think of to get a child to exhibit some responsible behavior, and nothing has made an impression on him, then it's time to seek professional help. But again, those cases are rare.

The Child Is Father of the Man

During the past several years I have had the occasion to do literally hundreds of lifestyle interpretations, and it is more and more apparent to me that adults behave in much the same way they did when they were little boys and girls. The little boy or girl you once were is still with you today in your adult life—unless some kind of therapeutic intervention or traumatic experience has occurred. The same will be true of your children.

If someone is an attention-getter at age 5, chances are he'll still be an attention-getter when he's 40. If he's into power-driven behavior as a child, chances are he'll be doing the same kinds of things to his wife and co-workers as an adult. If someone is a perfectionist as a child, she is likely to be a perfectionist when she's nearing retirement age.

As we see negative life themes or lifestyles begin to develop in a child, it's important to take corrective action so that the child will see himself in better and more positive terms. His entire life is at stake.

Exercise

• As you go back through this chapter, try to determine what lifestyles you see taking shape in the lives of your children. If you see negative ones, list several things you can and will do to change the situation.

• Have you ever thought about all the ways your children differ from one another? Spend some time making a list of those differences. Then pledge that, with God's help, you will encourage your children in their differences, that you will not expect them to act alike, and that you will not compare them to one another.

• Resolve that the next time your child throws a tantrum, or tries to demonstrate his power by acting in some unacceptable way, you will calmly remove him from your presence and allow him to continue his behavior where no one else will be bothered by it.

7

The First Thing
I Remember...

What's the first thing you remember?

Close your eyes and think. Go back... back... way back. I
don't mean to sound mystical, but I do want you to try to
remember the very first scene that comes to mind from your
childhood. It may be that there isn't one particular event, but
rather a series of events that can't be placed into chronologi-
cal order.

Taking a look at your earliest memories is a particularly
good indicator of the way you feel about yourself. Asking your
child about his memories can give you a pretty clear idea of
the lifestyle he is developing, and of how he sees his relationship with you.

For example, consider one of the earliest memories of
evangelist Billy Graham, who can recall back much further
than most of us. He remembers his father trying to get him to
take his first few steps. They were in a grassy field not far from

their house, and Billy's dad was clapping his hands, opening his arms and saying, "Come to daddy, c'mon to daddy."

With an earliest memory like that, it's no wonder Billy Graham was able, very early in life, to develop a deep and loving relationship with God. It was easy for him to see God as a loving Father who has his arms open wide and says, "Come to daddy." No wonder he has been so effective at bringing others into a relationship with God.

It's interesting to note that as he was growing up, Billy Graham did not have that good of a relationship with his father. Yet those earliest memories suggest he was developing a lifestyle of trust and commitment.

Now, what about the fellow whose earliest memories are of being extremely rebellious in school, often angry and cursing his teachers, and running out of the schoolyard? This defiant youth became a rebellious adult. In fact, he led a revolution that overthrew his nation's government. His name is Fidel Castro.

Unfortunately, another incident in young Castro's life involved him tripping and falling as he ran one afternoon, somehow getting a nail stuck in his tongue. When his mother found out about it, she told him that was God's punishment for cursing his teachers.

He believed it, at least for awhile, and maybe he still does. Maybe that's part of the reason he embraced godless communism so passionately and now refuses to give in to change—even when the rest of the world is acknowledging communism does not work.

A couple more earliest memories before we move on. Carol Burnett, who lives to make people laugh, remembers, "Being bathed in the kitchen sink in the old house. I couldn't have been much over 2, because I fit in. Mama kept the door on the stove open, and I'd stare at the waves in the air the heat made. I remember her drying me, holding me, kissing me, and putting me to bed. It felt good."

Carol Burnett's early life was no fairy tale. Her father had a drinking problem, and she was finally left behind to stay with a grandmother when her parents moved out of state.

Remember, however, that whether earliest memories are pleasant or negative may have little relation to life as it really existed at the time. Out of the millions of possible recollections a person could have, his memory selects the ones that are most in agreement with his lifestyle. It could be that 70 percent of the things that happened to him were good, but all of his earliest memories are negative, indicating some deep-seated problems. Conversely, it could be that 70 percent of what happened to him was negative, but his subconscious has chosen to remember things that are happy, meaning he has developed a rather healthy lifestyle in spite of everything. This is the Law of Creative Consistency: The memories your subconscious chooses to retain most vividly will show a clear relationship to your lifestyle.

With that in mind, guess who borrowed all his brother's blocks, promising to return them when he was through with them? The only problem was, he liked what he built so much that he glued it all together and never returned the blocks. If you said "Donald Trump," give yourself 10 points. That was the very beginning of all his wheelings and dealings.

Or what about the fellow who remembers waiting outside the supermarket door with his little red wagon, offering to help people cart their groceries home—for a tip, of course. His name is Lee Iacocca, and he is one of the movers and shakers of American industry.

Talking to Your Children About Memories

Most kids love to talk about the past. A fondness for nostalgia seems to be inherent to the human race. Even a 6-year-old child loves to talk about the "old days," when he was a baby.

Why are early memories so important? Part of the reason is that a child is making a great many decisions about life in the first 5 or 6 years of life.

He's deciding who he is. He's figuring out what life is all about. He's deciding what he likes and what he doesn't like. He's also coming to an understanding of what's good and what's bad, and the differences between the two. He's developing an attitude about God.

At this point in a child's life, everything is new. There is wide-eyed wonder at every adventure and experience. His life is like a blank slate upon which rules of living are being written. And, as a parent, you are for the most part the one who determines what is going to be inscribed upon that slate.

When you talk to your child about earliest childhood memories, it's important that you let the child tell you what he remembers. Don't try to lead him through the process. If you say, "Julie, do you remember that time when...?" then you're the one bringing up the memory, not the child. Yes, the child may clearly remember the event you're talking about, but he may not have recalled it without your mentioning it. An important memory to you, whether good or bad, may not have made much of an impression on the child.

That is another reason why exploring earliest memories will be beneficial to you. You may be relieved to discover that some things you feel very bad about don't even rank in your child's top 50 memories.

For example, I know a woman who felt very guilty about an incident that occurred in the grocery store when her little boy was 3. She had him sitting in the grocery cart, and as she turned away to look for some dishwashing liquid, he decided to reach out for the Lucky Charms cereal on the other side of the aisle. He couldn't reach that far, so he decided to stand up. The next thing mom heard was a loud crash, as little Bernard dived head-first onto the floor.

The little boy was bumped and bruised, but wasn't seriously hurt. As for poor mom, however, it took years to get over her feelings of guilt. How could she have let her little boy take a swan-dive onto the floor like that?

Believe it or not, when mom questioned Bernard, who was now 10, about his earliest memories, the grocery-store incident didn't even come up. Finally, when she asked him if he remembered falling out of the grocery cart, he laughed and said, "Oh yeah. I really wanted those Lucky Charms."

It was a painful incident, to be sure, but the memory wasn't painful at all. Mom was relieved because she figured she had probably scarred her son's psyche, not to mention his hard little head, for the rest of his life. In fact, nothing of the sort had really happened.

On the other hand, you may discover some events you considered quite harmless, that you had long ago forgotten, play a prominent part in your child's attitudes about life.

You may also find out about an incident you knew had been significant in your child's life at some point "long ago," but which you assumed had been pushed out of his mind by now.

For example, when my daughter Holly was 4 years old, she went grocery shopping with her mother one day. Because it was near the store's closing time and the manager wanted to alert everyone to that fact, he turned off the lights for just a moment. They weren't off long, but long enough to put terror into a little girl's heart.

Not long ago, Holly, who is now in college, and I were doing some shopping. We hurried into a department store—just before closing time—to get the last item on our list. As we walked in, I saw Holly look at her watch and glance around anxiously to see what was going on.

It's not that she was really afraid the lights would be turned off. It wouldn't scare her today the way it did when she was 4. But she still carries the memory of that terrifying incident from so long ago, and she remembers the feeling she had when those lights were turned off.

That is an insignificant incident to be sure, but it made a lasting impression on Holly. It's likely she will never be able to be in a store around closing time without feeling at least a twinge of anxiety.

Getting the Discussion Started

Here are some questions you can use to discover what predominant memories play a part in your child(ren)'s life. If you have several children, encourage all of them to join in your discussion. Going over memories is not only a good way to bring out hidden perceptions and attitudes, but it can also strengthen relationships as your family relives good times they have had together.

1. Can you remember any special things that happened to you when you were small?
2. What's your earliest memory?
3. How did what happened that day make you feel?
4. How do you feel now, looking back on what happened that day?
5. How would you have changed the situation if you could have?

6. What is the clearest part of that memory?
7. Would you like to go back to that day and do it all over again?
8. Why, or why not?
9. What was I doing at the time?
10. Did you feel in control of the situation?
11. Did you feel helpless?
12. What are some of the other earliest memories you have?

You can ask these questions, or variations on them, for each of the memories your children share. From the child's answers, you can get a pretty good idea of the lifestyle he is developing. And you can also see how he perceives you as a parent. Remember, if you or your spouse do not come out so well in some of these memories, this is definitely not the time to have hurt feelings or blame the child for having a bad attitude. The key is to uncover how the child perceives things—whether that perception is right or wrong—and then work to improve the situation.

One bit of advice: Try not to make the child think you are prying or psychoanalyzing him. If there are several children, let them take turns sharing their memories. Perhaps you will want to give a few memories of your own. The idea is to make it a fun experience, a game. If a child doesn't want to talk about it right now, don't push. Wait until he's ready.

As a child tells you about his earliest memories, you may begin to see a pattern emerge. You should be able to begin to see:

• How your child perceives you.
• How he sees himself.
• How he sees other members of the family.
• How he relates to people—or perhaps more accurately, why he relates to people the way he does.

- How he sees the world around him.
- How he perceives God.

Ask yourself, are his memories predominantly:

- Happy.
- Sad.
- Angry.
- Fearful.

Does he most vividly remember times when he was:

- Losing?
- Winning?
- With others?
- By himself?

What Should I Do Next?

The next question is, what do you do with all this information about early memories once you've got it?

1. *Do a little "remodeling."*

The first thing you need to know is that *memories can be rewritten.*

For example, perhaps your child has misunderstood some of the things that have happened in his life. Perhaps he heard you talking about one thing, but thought you were talking about him. Maybe his feelings were hurt, or his safety was threatened, and that incident still bothers him.

You can say to him, "You know what was really happening that day, don't you?" Spend some time talking about how you can make that memory better. "The next time you think about that, try to remember it *this* way."

Not only can you work on clearing up any misunderstandings on the child's part, you can begin to remodel memories where bad things really did happen. Although you may not be able to make bad things actually look good to him, you can undergird those memories with love. For example, in Holly's situation my wife could assure her, "You know honey, I was right there beside you when the lights went off in that supermarket. I wouldn't have let anything happen to you." What you want to do is take the edge off the bad memories, and make them a little easier on the subconscious.

2. *Set out to make some good memories.*

It is inevitable that a few of your child's earliest memories aren't going to be good. It's also inevitable that you are going to play the bad guy in the few of these incidents. There may have been times when the child felt you weren't listening to him, when you punished him unjustly, or when you were an "old meany" because you wouldn't let him do something or other. (Yes, it may have resulted in the house being blown to bits if you had let him do it, but all he can see is that "mean ol' mom" kept him from having a good time.)

Well, unless you are the villain in nearly every one of your child's memories, don't berate yourself for being the bad guy. There will always be misunderstandings, and even the best parents in the world goof up once in awhile.

But beyond talking to your child about those memories and trying to explain things from your point of view, the best thing you can do is move on to the future. Resolve to make some special memories. Now I'm not talking about over-indulging the child—just doing some things that will create happy memories for years to come.

For example, I strongly suggest parents spend some quality one-on-one time with every child in the family. If you have 12 kids, it may not be that easy, but you can do it. Ask the child what he would like to do, and then take a Saturday or Sunday afternoon and do it with him. (Unless, that is, the kid tells you he's always wanted to go hang gliding over the Grand Canyon, or something equally as "thrilling.") Maybe he'll want to go see a movie, spend an afternoon at the park, go horseback riding, etc. By doing what he really wants to do, and demonstrating your love for him in that way, you're building good, new memories to take precedence over the old, bad ones. And that means you're remodeling his attitude about life, too.

Does your family go on vacations together? Have you spent some time in an amusement park lately? Do you celebrate special occasions like birthdays?

All of these things help build those vitally important happy memories. Remember, one or two of these good memories may be so important that they alter the child's entire approach to life!

3. *Put the good memories to work for you.*

Don't concentrate on bad memories. The good ones are just as important, because they give incidents where your child demonstrated excellent character, behaved in a way that made you especially proud of him, and so on.

Spend some time talking about the good memories with your child. Give him positive reinforcement so he knows that you care about him and appreciate the good things he has done. Saying something like, "I remember that, and I felt very happy that you did that," will help reinforce the child's positive behavior and attitude. Be careful not to convey the feeling that you were proud of the child *only* because he behaved in a certain way. You're proud of him because of who he is—your child—but you can let him know it makes you happy when he behaves properly or shows particular strength of character.

Children really do want to please their parents, although I know some people find that hard to believe. The fact is, they will *usually* turn to the peer group for approval only if they feel they cannot get it from their parents. They will not begin to do things to purposefully displease their parents unless: 1) it's the only way they know how to get the attention they want, or 2) they are after revenge.

Even negative memories may have some positive aspects you can use to help the child, such as:

- "You were very brave, weren't you?"
- "I would have reacted just the way you did."
- "Yes, I felt very bad about that, and I'm sorry it happened."

See what you're doing here? In the first instance, you're making the child feel good about his own behavior, even though the memory itself might be bad or scary. In the second instance you're letting him know he's not a "goof." Telling him you would have handled it exactly the way he did makes him feel better about his choices, and it is also likely to strengthen communication between the two of you. In the third example, you're apologizing for something that *was* your fault. It's not easy for a parent to say, "I'm sorry, I was wrong," but it's important. I strongly urge you to try it next time you're wrong.

4. *Take a look at your parenting skills.*

As you listen to your child's earliest memories you should begin to see, from his perspective, how you are doing as a mother or father.

There are many types of parents, but they fall into three basic categories: authoritarian, permissive, and authoritative. The authoritarian parent rules with an iron hand. His word is law; he's right even when he's wrong, and he doesn't listen to the child's point of view. He doesn't think he needs to. The permissive parent is just the opposite. Whatever his child wants is okay with him. If there's an inch to give he'll give it, because the last thing he wants is a confrontation. The authoritative parent is balanced between the two extremes.

He sets clear boundaries for the children, and expects them to obey. At the same time, he is willing to listen to their point of view, and may even change his mind once in awhile. He won't, however, give in just because he's tired of hearing about it. He'll give in because he decides he's been wrong and the children have been right. When he knows he's been wrong he admits it.

If you are a permissive parent, you are likely going to see this aspect of your personality replayed in your children's memories. You may see times when bad situations developed because you should have said no and didn't. Or times when you let your children manipulate you because you wanted them to like you and not be angry with you.

If you are an authoritarian parent, you will see times when your children were hurt because you refused to listen to their point of view. You may even see times when you said or did something that was cruel, for which you need to apologize.

Again...let me assure you...no parents are perfect. Most of us are authoritarian on one occasion and then permissive on another, as we try to walk the line down the middle of the highway. It may be that you will see you have been much too strict. It may be that you will see you have been much too relaxed and permissive. More than likely, you will see there have been times you've wobbled all over the place. What you want to do is improve your parenting skills so you can be consistently authoritative—so that your children will not feel like yo-yos. They need to know mom or dad is always going to be firm, but fair.

What can you do if you see you are too permissive? Constantly remind yourself, "My responsibility is to love my children, and I can sometimes demonstrate that love best through discipline. I must and will confront and discipline them when they need it." Do your best to parent your children, with that in mind.

If you see you have been an authoritarian parent, remind yourself, "I can be in authority over my children without squashing or suffocating them. I can and will take the time to show I am aware of and interested in their feelings. I will take the time to explain my actions."

Exercises

• If you are doing something as a parent that you know is wrong, stop to think about it. Resolve to handle the situation another way.

• Don't be afraid to apologize to your child when you've made a mistake.

• Spend some time working on "remodeling" your children's memories.

• Spend even more time making beautiful memories for tomorrow.

Responsibility Training

*M*ost parents readily agree that responsibility training for children is necessary. However, as we pointed out earlier, parents, school, and society in general often do a beautiful job of teaching *irresponsibility* instead.

One of the biggest problems parents face is arguing and fighting among siblings who don't know how to behave responsibly toward each other. I realize that even the best-behaved and most loving brothers and sisters will go at it every once in awhile, but some kids are constantly at each other's throats. What do you do when you have a situation like that in the family?

When mom and dad first brought Ronnie and Rickie to me, Ronnie was 10 and Rickie was 9. They went at each other like a couple of professional wrestlers trying to work an audience. Not only did this fighting cause lots of headaches for the parents, but Ronnie was much bigger than his brother,

141

and Rickie often got hurt. Even when these boys weren't fighting physically, they were always cutting each other down, trying to outdo one another when it came to insults.

I told mom and dad there was no way they could really stop the fighting, since children have a right to fight with one another if that's what they choose to do. I also told them fighting is really an expression of cooperation, since it takes "two to tango." Having two children who fight is better than having one child who constantly picks on the other.

It wasn't easy, but I convinced mom and dad it was in the family's best interest to let the children experience the consequences of their choosing to fight. Mom especially was afraid the younger boy would get hurt if she didn't rush in to "referee," as she was always doing. I told her to let Rickie fend for himself. If he wound up hurt, he would at least understand what would happen if he persisted in his behavior.

We also discussed some necessary guidelines. For example, fighting was not to be permitted in the house. Although we agreed the children had a right to fight, they could only fight outside, where the peace of mom and dad would not be disturbed. Mom and dad were told that any time the children chose to fight they were to be escorted out of the house, preferably into the backyard, with instructions to let the parents know when the fight was over.

At our fourth counseling session, dad came in with an irrepressible smile on his face. He told me the two boys had had a shaving-cream war while in the bathtub.

He said, "I remembered your words. You instructed us to use action!"

That's exactly what dad did. He went in , grabbed both boys by the arm, pulled them out of the bathtub soaking wet, and put them outside. Well, you can imagine that the fight didn't last very long. Both boys were terribly embarrassed and couldn't wait to get back in the house. That war was quickly over! (Yes, the backyard was fenced, in case anybody thinks dad went too far.)

One thing mom and dad discovered was that the boys began to fight less frequently since they knew their parents would not intervene. If mom and dad didn't really care if the boys fought, then it just plain wasn't that much fun.

Now if one of the boys gets hurt and runs to mom and dad they say, "We're sure you can handle it!" Before, when the same thing happened, there had been a sharp lecture about fighting, and then mom or dad would coddle the injured party. All of this, instead of helping diffuse the situation, actually encouraged it to happen again.

Children usually choose to fight in front of adults, or at least when adults are close at hand. They want someone to be there to break it up before any damage is done. That's why they often choose the hallway of a school to go at it, where an adult will come along in a matter of minutes. I've had teachers tell me that when they've given children the opportunity to fight in the gymnasium with boxing gloves on, without anyone to watch, they usually back down. It usually goes something like this:

"Come on, man, you start it."

"No...you start it."

"No...come on...take a poke at me."

"Oh...I don't really want to fight you."

"Uh...me neither."

And it's all over.

If your children always seem to be fighting, remember that one of their primary reasons is to get your attention—to get you involved in their squabbles. You, as a parent, have much better things to do than spend your time wearing a uniform that consists of a striped shirt and whistle.

Discipline by Isolation

I believe the greatest disciplinary measure a parent of pre-teen children can develop is the use of isolation— putting a child out of the home for a period of time with the understanding he can come back in once the unacceptable behavior has stopped. What do you do, for instance, when little Egbert throws a tantrum right in the middle of mom and dad's favorite TV show? Simply pick him up and put him outside. Let him throw his tantrum there, where you don't have to be bothered by it. I am not saying a television show should take precedence over your child. The child needs to understand however, that this is something mommy and daddy want to do, and they don't want to be bothered unless it's an emergency. It is vitally important that husbands and wives protect their time together, and that the children be taught to respect it.

What do you do if you're on the phone with an important call and Elberta starts interrupting you every few seconds, even though you've told her you can't talk to her right now? The same thing. Pick her up and put her outside the door until she's ready to behave, or at least until your call is over.

Be careful, though, not to forget the child is out there. That's what one mother did. She told me she was on the phone and her little boy and girl would not stop interrupting. The more she asked them to be quiet, the louder and more obnoxious they became. She had heard me speak at a seminar and knew my advice in these situations, so she scooped up the kids, deposited them on the patio, and locked the sliding glass doors behind them. Then she went back to her phone call.

After she finished the call she forgot what she had done with the kids. The house seemed quiet and peaceful, and that certainly should have reminded her, but she went about her housework for a time. She enjoyed the fact that her children were playing so peacefully. About 30 minutes later when she went into the den to get something, she noticed two little faces pressed up against the glass, pleading to come back in.

She felt bad that she'd forgotten about them for so long, especially because, "It was kind of cold out there." But you know what? Those children were very well behaved for the rest of the day, and they learned a valuable lesson as to "Who's in charge here?"

The fact that it was cold that day brings up a question I am often asked. "What if it's cold outside?"

Well, if it's *really* cold, if it's raining or threatening snow or below freezing, then perhaps you would want to put the child in his room rather than outside. Most of the time, however, it will be perfectly all right to put the child outside. It's unlikely he'll be out there for more than a few minutes anyway, and remember, he can come back in as soon as he decides to behave. All he has to do is knock on the door and tell you he's ready to act as he should.

I had one mother ask, "Would it be all right if I stopped and put my child's snowsuit on before I put her outside?"

My answer? Well, that kind of takes the edge off things, doesn't it? By the time that mother has all the buttons buttoned and the zippers zipped, she and the child will have forgotten what this was all about in the first place. The action needs to be swift and decisive. The child has to understand mommy and daddy mean business, and that this type of behavior will not be tolerated.

I have had some people suggest that putting a child outside for a few minutes sounds almost as bad as locking a child in a closet. I'm sorry, but I fail to see any connection whatsoever. Being put into a closet where it is cramped and dark can be terrifying for a child. There is nothing terrifying about being put outside. Being put in a closet instills fear into the child's heart. He knows he'd better behave or he will have something awful done to him. Being put outside *until he tells you he's ready to behave* does not cause the child to fear, but clearly shows him there are certain behaviors you will not tolerate.

What About Spanking?

I am often asked how I feel about spanking. Over the years I have become more and more convinced spanking is an effective way of disciplining a child if—and this is a major if—it is done properly.

Spanking should never be done in anger, as a means of releasing the parent's emotions. And when I say "spanking," I'm referring to a few swats on the child's bottom with the hand. I would never approve of hitting the child with a belt, a paddle, a brush, or anything of the sort. When mom or dad finds it necessary to administer a spanking, it should be given with the same hand that is used to help the child get across a busy street. After all, it is all part of the same business of safely guiding the child into adulthood.

The other thing I need to say about spanking is that it should be applied to the child's bottom, where it may hurt a little bit, but where there is sufficient "padding" to protect the child. Just as I would never spank a child with anything but the human hand, I would never hit him on the face or the hand. If you feel a spanking is called for, be sure you get to "the bottom of the matter."

A swat or two on a child's bottom can be a very good disciplinary measure, especially in situations where the child's safety is in question. Suppose you looked out the window and saw your 2-year-old playing in the street. Once you got him out of the street, a swat on his bottom would be a very good reminder that this behavior is a definite "no-no." But swats always need to be followed up with honest communication, expressing love and concern for the child in a most intimate way.

To recap, here are three important things good parents remember and practice with regard to spanking: 1) They never spank their children in anger. 2) They never spank them unnecessarily hard or long—a few swats with an open hand, across the bottom. 3) They never play the "Wait until your father gets home" game. For any disciplinary action to be effective, it must be done *right now*, so it is closely connected in the child's mind to the offending behavior.

Let the Child Pay His Debts

Billy, who was 11, got a new 10-speed bike for his birthday. Along with it came some guidelines and added responsibilities concerning its use and care. He was not to ride on major streets, nor was he to leave his bike out in the yard. It always had to be put away in the garage if he was not riding it. Dad made clear to Billy that if he did not abide by the rules, that shiny new bike would be taken away from him.

The first violation of those rules brought a stern warning and a reminder from dad about what would happen the next time. The second violation meant that dad put a "for sale" sign on the bike and put it out in the front yard. After just three days, somebody bought it.

Billy was heartbroken, of course. And dad and mom were both tempted to give in and change their minds. But they knew they couldn't. Having a bike like that was a big responsibility, and Billy had to show them he was capable of handling it.

Billy wanted to know what would happen if he bought his own bike. Dad replied that would be fine, but he would still have to abide by those important rules.

Billy was anxious to get that bike back so he spent the next two months working—cutting lawns and doing yard work and chores in the neighborhood to earn enough money to buy his own bike. Once he got it, you can bet he took care of it. He locked it up at night, made sure it was treated properly, and didn't ride it where he wasn't supposed to.

Billy's dad had done something that was very difficult for a parent to do. Yet through his actions, he had held Billy accountable for not following family guidelines. As tough as it was for both the boy and his father, they both profited from dad's responsible parenting.

I was working with a family in a parent education center several years ago when I met a boy named Johnny, who was 10 years old. He had an 8-year-old sister named Tracey, and their mom was very much into entertaining in their lovely home in the foothills. Johnny had one primary responsibility each week—cutting the lawn on Thursday evenings. Johnny was a good kid, but he was also absent-minded. He always had excuses for why his one chore was not completed.

I told him that from now on if he didn't cut the lawn when he was supposed to, mom and dad would pay someone else to cut it for him. His eyes lit up. I could see he was planning to forget about the lawn this coming Thursday. But when I said, "And guess who's going to pay for it?" his mouth flew open in disbelief.

The plan was simple. If Johnny had not cut the lawn by 5 P.M. on Thursday, mom was to go next door and ask the 14-year-old boy who lived there if he would cut the lawn. His fee would be deducted from Johnny's allowance. Well, we didn't have to wait too many Thursdays before Johnny stayed too long at the playground and didn't get home until well past lawn-cutting time.

When Johnny didn't show up, mom went next door, but the boy wasn't home. By this time Tracey was jumping up and down at the prospect of earning some extra money. She said she would love to mow the lawn. Mom wasn't sure if Tracey could handle it, but finally decided to let her try. And she did a good job.

After Johnny finally came home, his little sister couldn't wait to tell him she had cut the lawn for him and, more importantly, that he owed her some money from his allowance. Johnny certainly wasn't happy about the situation, but he most definitely learned his lesson. He never missed another lawn-mowing appointment.

By holding Johnny accountable for his actions, and giving him the choice of doing the work himself or paying someone else to do it for him, his parents were really helping to prepare Johnny for life. After all, that's the way it works out there in the "real world," isn't it?

Another illustration comes to mind.

I received a phone call one night from a friend who was a strong, committed Christian and a leader in his church. He was extremely upset because he discovered his daughter had stolen a pack of cigarettes from a supermarket and had taken them to school. In addition to smoking a few herself, she had sold the rest of them for 10 cents each. Dad was upset because she was stealing, smoking, and then involving other girls in her "crime." He wanted to know what he should do about it.

I asked him what he had done so far. He replied that he had talked to his daughter, and told her she had broken the state law and also God's moral law.

"Well, what did you do then?" I asked.

"It was 10 o'clock at night, and I really didn't know what to do. That's why I'm calling you."

As we continued to talk, I asked him again to tell me who stole the cigarettes.

"Judy."

"Then what needs to be done?"

He replied, "She should pay for the cigarettes."

I said, "Right. What else needs to be done?"

"Well, she should probably take the cigarettes back to the store."

I said, "Yes, there's your answer. You solved it yourself. She needs to be held accountable. She needs to go back to the store, pay the manager for the cigarettes, and return the unused ones."

The next day, Judy's dad drove her to the store. Then he waited in the car as his 12-year-old daughter went in to face the music. Now I don't know what school of psychology they send supermarket managers to, but it must be a pretty good one. This man spent about 10 minutes with the girl, explaining how shoplifting affected the store and the consumer. His talk really seemed to register with her. As far as dad's role he hadn't done any lecturing or putting Judy down. He had simply demonstrated responsible parenting as he assisted his daughter in taking the action she needed to take.

I realize it is tempting to rush to a child's rescue, even when it's his own fault that he finds himself in a mess. However, it is counterproductive to do so.

What About Lying?

They say George Washington never told a lie. I, for one, don't believe it. I've never known a child who didn't tell a lie at some time or another.

But why? And what can a parent do when he knows his child is lying?

The answer to the first question is that children usually tell lies for one of two reasons. Number one, because they wish something were so that isn't, they just say it *is* so. Sometimes they know they're lying. Sometimes, however, they get confused between what is real and what is pretend, and they have to be reminded about what is true.

This "wish fulfillment" is what is at work when your 4-year-old tells the neighbor, "My daddy keeps a pair of wings in the trunk of the car. And sometimes when we're going somewhere, he puts the wings on and we fly." It may also be what's causing your little girl to tell her friends at school that The New Kids on The Block came to her birthday party last year.

The second reason for lying is fear. The child is afraid that if he tells the truth, he's going to get in trouble. He certainly doesn't want to get in trouble, so he lies. Thus your child may tell you he's getting an A in math when he knows full well he's getting a D. He also knows you'll discover the truth sooner or later, but he figures later is the better of the two alternatives.

What you can do about lying? The first and most important thing is to try to see things from the child's perspective, so you can understand why he told the lie. Is there a reason he would be afraid to come to you with the truth? Does he create lies to make himself sound big and important because the things that happen to him in reality make him feel small and insignificant? I'm not suggesting you condone your child's lying—just that you do whatever you can to get at the underlying reason.

Your child should be confronted about his lying, of course. When you do confront, however, it helps if you can say, "I think I know why you lied to me, and it's this. Am I right?"

By telling the child you believe you know the reason for his untruthfulness, you are opening the door to further communication. Don't just say, "You lied to me, so I'm going to punish you." It is important that you get to the bottom of the problem.

I have had parents tell me they will not discipline a child for a lie if the truth comes out without much prodding. This is a good position to take. What you want to do is show the child the importance of telling the truth—not make him feel his lies just have to be *better* next time.

You can say something like, "Jenny, you lied to me and when you lie, you should be punished. Yet because you've told me the truth now, I'm not going to punish you. But I don't want you to lie again. The next time I catch you lying, I'm going to make you stay in your room all afternoon,"—or some such disciplinary measure.

Suppose your child was bouncing a ball in the house, which you've told him not to do, and he broke your favorite lamp. At first he tries to blame the family dog, but then, after a little prodding on your part, admits what really happened. Does that mean you don't punish him for breaking your rule not to play ball in the house, because he was a good boy and told the truth?

No, not at all. You need to make clear that the violation of the first rule must bring discipline. Your child also needs to see, however, that lying would have made things much worse. Let him know that since he so quickly told you the truth, you're not going to give him any extra punishment for the lie. He must see that honesty is always the best policy.

Another course of action you can take is to hold the child accountable for his lies. Suppose your son promised everybody that Joe Montana was coming to his birthday party, and now he's really on the spot. Some parents would be tempted to try to get Joe Montana to come to the party—just so their son wouldn't be embarrassed. That's the wrong approach. The right approach is to have the boy call his friends, one at a time, and tell them he lied about Joe Montana. Would it be difficult for a parent to make his son do something like that? You bet it would. But it is the very best way to deal with lying.

Warning: Jungle Room Ahead

If you've ever been to Graceland, Elvis Presley's home in Memphis, you know that he had a Jungle Room in the house. It was a really "wild" place.

Well, as impressed as I was by that at first, I finally realized that, hey, it's no big deal. Just about any house in America where there are kids has at least one or two jungle rooms! It's very likely that you know what I'm talking about. The room is often such a mess that an elephant could be hiding in there somewhere, and you wouldn't be able to see it!

In most homes, the cleaning and picking up of kids' bedrooms is a major source of hassles between parents and children. How often have you said something like, "I don't know how you can stand it in here," only to have the child shoot back with, "I like it this way!" What can you do about the constant battle to get your children to keep their rooms neat—or at least orderly enough that you don't have to hire a safari guide to find your way around?

Well, there are essentially two views on the subject. The first is that the room belongs to the child and that he or she should be entirely responsible for it. That means the parents do not have to straighten the room, nor should they ever enter it for any reason, even changing the sheets or picking up dirty clothes. The other view is that the child's room is part of the household, and should be kept clean like the rest of the home. I generally agree with the second perspective.

A child needs to learn to be accountable for himself. It's important that we parents don't do things for children they can do for themselves. If clothes don't get put in the hamper, then they don't get washed and the children have to wear them dirty. When the Little Leaguer's uniform isn't clean and bright the way he wants it, then he has to live with the consequences. If Susie's dress isn't ready for her special party because she forgot to put it in the hamper, then she has to wear another one.

I've had parents go to the extreme of throwing away anything they find lying around. If the child wants it back, he can go out and dig through the garbage. This kind of action obviously takes real commitment on the part of parents.

One father told me he had a particularly hard time getting his 13-year-old daughter to clean her room. The place just about always looked like the aftermath of an earthquake, and was a constant source of friction between them.

What the father finally decided to do—which I think was a pretty good idea—was draw up a contract that he and his daughter both signed. It stipulated that the girl's room was to be thoroughly cleaned, at least once a week, prior to 5 P.M. on Fridays. The contract spelled out specific penalties if the room was not cleaned by that time, and further penalties to accrue until the room was cleaned.

What it boiled down to was this: If the girl expected to have a good time over the weekend with her friends, her room had better be cleaned. In the meantime, mom and dad didn't nag her. Her room could be as messy as she wanted it and they were not allowed to say a word about it. That was also in the contract.

Of course, the girl soon learned that the neater she kept the room during the week, the easier it was to clean it up on Friday. And, incidentally, this was no cleanup where the dirt could be swept under the rug and dirty clothes thrown into the closet. The room had to pass inspection.

In addition, the contract prevented the daughter's groaning and moaning about her parents being unfair. If she failed to clean her room, all her parents had to do was show her the contract. All in all, it not only resulted in a generally tidier room, but it went a long way toward eliminating family friction.

How old would a child have to be before he could understand and be held to a contract like that? It depends on the child, but generally children who are only 6 or 7 years old can understand the importance of keeping such a promise.

Should You Pay Children For Chores?

While we're on the subject of children's rooms, let's move on to the realm of household chores in general. Specifically, I am often asked whether a child should be paid for helping out around the house.

Now I realize there are occasions when a major chore needs to be done or a child needs money for a particular reason, but I generally discourage parents from paying children to do chores. Chores are a part of any child's responsibility in the home. Because he reaps the benefits of being a family member, each child needs to have responsibilities that genuinely help mom, dad, and other family members.

I believe every child within the family should be assigned certain tasks to perform weekly, simply as part of his duty to the family. However, if Billy sees a new baseball glove he really wants, I don't see anything wrong with finding some extra jobs he can do around the house to make money. Perhaps he can pull weeds, rake leaves, wash the car, or do some other little extras to earn the cash he needs.

Along with the notion of chores and accountability comes the privilege of having an allowance. I believe each child in the family ought to have some money to spend the way he sees fit. Allowances are probably the greatest thing going for parents, and yet I encounter many people who fight the notion of giving them. To those parents opposed, I challenge them to count the dollars they spend on their children every week. When they do, they're usually surprised to find out that giving a regular allowance would save them quite a bit—as long as they explain to the child that the allowance is his money for the week. Once he's spent it, there won't be any more until next week.

Of course, I think the child should be taught to use money you give him wisely, no matter how much it is. He should try to save some, put a portion into the offering plate at church or Sunday school, and so on. Maybe you would even want to help your child draw up a budget. Some parents tell their children they will double the money the child puts into a savings account. Or, suppose your child wants to buy something that costs $20. He feels it will take him forever to save that long, so he's thinking about giving up. You can tell him that if he will save until he has $10, you'll give him the rest. Either way, you're getting the child into the habit of saving a portion of his money, and teaching him that saving to buy something "big" is possible.

As I mentioned earlier, I believe that if specific chores are not done by an agreed-upon time, mom or dad, as the money managers in the home, may request someone else to do them. If another child does them, he ought to get paid for the specific jobs, and the money ought to come from the original child's allowance. Holding a child accountable for doing a particular task, or else paying for the privilege of having somebody else do it for him, is really what life will require of him.

Bedtime and Other Hassles

Another problem area in many households is bedtime. Now it's easy to send the children off to bed at the same time, particularly if they are close in age, but extreme caution needs to be exercised here. The birthright effect should be in full force. The older the child, the longer he ought to be allowed to stay up. A 15-minute difference can really make a significant change in the behavior of children.

There also needs to be a set of routines involved with bedtime, particularly with younger children. For example, a child may have one treat, one drink, and one story before his bedtime. Then, once he's tucked in and prayers have been said, if he gets out of the bed for any reason, he should have to forego the privilege of having mom or dad tuck him back in.

A child who balks at going to bed can be asked, "Do you want to be carried to bed or walk to bed yourself? You decide." Limiting choices is a good skill for parents to learn. Notice in this situation you did not give the child the option of staying up for another half-hour. He has options, but both of them lead back to the bed.

The dinner hour, too, is a needless battleground in many homes. Parents tell their kids what to eat and how to eat it, when that really ought to be a decision the child makes. Food should be put before the child, giving him the choice of eating it or not eating it. If the child chooses not to eat, there's no need to lecture. Simply remove the food from the table and dismiss the child. But mom shouldn't make the child a peanut butter sandwich just because the little darling doesn't like the gourmet dinner it took six hours to prepare! If the child doesn't like what's for dinner, he'll have to go to bed hungry.

So, parents, save all those stories about starving children in other parts of the world. I've never seen a child who was convinced to eat broccoli by one of those stories anyway.

If a child is late for dinner, the consequence ought to be that he serves his own dinner, or else goes without it. There should be no special attention or catering by mom and dad in this situation, unless, or course, the child's tardiness is caused by a reason beyond his control.

Another major family hassle can be created by pets. Many times I find parents buy a pet for their child without the child really expressing a desire for it. Then these same parents have difficulty getting the child to care for the pet.

However, if a child has really wanted a pet and yet ends up neglecting it, the consequence should be that the pet is sold or given to a family where it will receive proper care. This is a good idea for the sake of the neglectful child, and the pet he is neglecting. Most parents aren't able to do this because it seems so "hard-hearted." They may threaten their children with taking away the pet if the situation doesn't improve, but they don't follow through. Such idle threats only teach children that mommy and daddy's words can be ignored because they don't really mean anything.

Remember, mom or dad, we need to expose children to responsibility training early in life so that when the demands of the teenage and adult years become reality, they will be prepared to make wise decisions. It's the seemingly minor responsibilities and challenges we give children in the early years that pay off handsomely at ages 16, 17, and 18—with responsible thinking and responsible behavior. A home needs to be a laboratory of life where mistakes are not only allowed but expected as well.

Commitment Is Crucial

The point is, until commitment comes from parents to effect behavioral change, change will not occur. Parents must give children the right to make decisions for themselves and then to be responsible for those decisions.

One of the most difficult things for a parent to do is just keep his or her mouth shut and not say anything. It's difficult because we're wiser, we have more knowledge, and we want to keep our children from experiencing the pain of failure. But the plain fact is that children need *the right to fail.* They need the right to fall flat on their faces every once in awhile.

The best parents are those who provide their children with an environment that says, "It's safe to try. It's safe to fail. And, if you fail, we'll help you pick yourself up, learn from it, and go on."

This is the same kind of environment that God provides for us as parents. We have the right to fail. As parents we're going to make many mistakes, yet God still loves us. He doesn't always like what we do. But He always loves us!

And we, as parents, will never find a better role model.

Exercises

• Call a family meeting and explain that you are instituting a new policy of "responsibility training." Explain to your children what this means—that they will be responsible for their own actions—for instance, that they will be called to the dinner table only once, and if they don't come when called, they will have to eat either a cold meal or do without.

159

Then, once this new family policy has been installed, stick to it!

• If your children are not already doing chores, assign each of them something to do to help out around the house. It can be as simple as keeping the dog's water dish full, but there is certainly something every child can do. This will add to the child's self-esteem, as well as give him a better understanding of his involvement in the upkeep of the home.

• Practice using these seven little words when dealing with quarrels between your children: "Honey, I'm sure you can handle it."

9

Games Kids (and Parents) Play

*C*hildren love games. You know that. Whether it's sports, video games, board games, or games like Kick the Can or Hide-n-Seek, it's great to see a bunch of kids playing together and having a good time.

But there are some children's games I don't care much for... games I see just about everyday in my private practice. These are the games that children are usually very adept at foisting on their parents. These are the games that parents need to learn how *not* to play, so their children can learn to behave responsibly. Remember, all of these games required the cooperation of the opposition for the encounter to be successful. By going along with them, parents ensure these needless games will persist. Let's take a look at a few, and discuss how *not* to play:

The Fighting-in-the-Car Game

This is an oldie but goodie. I think it used to be referred

to as "The Fighting-in-the-Covered-Wagon Game."

The car is a good place for children to draw parents into their hassles because it provides such *close quarters*. Dad drives down the highway, trying to steer with one hand while he breaks up the fight in the back seat with the other. Meanwhile, the kids accuse each other of horrible crimes against humanity such as "She *touched* me!" If you've ever taken a cross-country trip with your family by car, you know how intense and terrifying this game can become.

One way you can deal with it is to simply pull over to the side of the road. If the fighting continues, the parents need to get out of the car calmly, allow their children to fight, and withdraw themselves from the situation. If the children are on their way to an important event, you can imagine how soon the fighting will subside. If you're on your way to an amusement park, for instance, you can say, "As soon as you're done fighting, we'll be on our way."

Or you can say, "If you don't stop fighting, we'll turn around and go home." Before you say anything like that, however, be sure you're prepared to do it. You must make good on your threats.

The Beat-the-System Game

This is an interesting game. It comes about when parents dictate the rules of the family without the necessary involvement of their children. For instance, Billy, who was 10, was instructed to make his bed every morning. If there was one thing Billy hated, however, it was making that bed. I remember his father telling me, "Boy, that Billy is something."

"What did he do?"

"Well, we told him he had to make his bed every morning, so the last few nights he has been sleeping on top of his bedspread. He just gets up in the morning and smooths out the wrinkles!"

Billy was playing the Beat-the-System Game for all he was worth. Dad told him he couldn't do that anymore, and the next morning he found the boy curled up in the bathtub in his sleeping bag.

You can avoid this game by making sure your children understand the rules and guidelines of the family and, where appropriate, involving them in deciding the guidelines. In case you think I'm advocating letting the children make their own rules, notice I said "where appropriate." You're still the one in charge.

Some time ago, I worked with a family where there were five children—two boys ages 12 and 10, and three teenage girls. I suggested that perhaps the family could meet on a regular basis, and that the kids could have some input as to the rules and regulations of the home. The kids jumped at the opportunity, but dad wasn't so sure about it.

"Do you mean each of the kids gets one vote—an equal vote to what my wife and I would get?" he asked. When I said yes, that was what I meant, he replied, "That's five votes for them and two for us."

I asked him to trust me, that the kids would become more responsible as responsibility was delegated to them.

The next week, he came into my office with a smirk on his face and I thought, "Oh, oh. Something must have gone wrong."

I was right. When I asked him about it he said, "Well, I'll tell you how things have gone. We used to have rules and regulations at our house regarding what time people had to be home at night. If they were going someplace unexpectedly, the children were required to call and let us know where they were and when they would be home. Well, during that first meeting that *you suggested,* they wiped out all of the rules."

I swallowed hard and asked dad if he would please stick with the agreement for just a little while longer. Perhaps we could make this poor decision on the children's part a learning experience.

At my suggestion, the following evening, mom failed to come home from work at her usual 5:30 P.M. At around 7 P.M., dad and the children began to make calls to her place of employment, friends, and relatives, but no one had seen her. As the hours continued to tick by, the kids panicked. They were scared about what could have happened to their mom, and dad seemed to be just as concerned as they were. Even the fake call to the police went ever-so-smoothly. Meanwhile, mom was tucked into a hide-a-bed at her father-in-law's home.

At 7:30 the next morning, mom walked into the house. You can bet the kids flew to her—hugging and kissing her, telling her how worried they had been, and asking her what had happened.

Mom just shrugged. "I thought that our meeting wiped out all the rules and regulations about what time we had to be home at night, and that we didn't have to call people and let them know where we were."

Jamie, the oldest daughter, called for an immediate family meeting. Right then and there, all five of the kids voted to reinstate the same rules they had wiped out just a few days prior. Why? Because they had the opportunity to see that the rules really were in the family's best interests.

Sure, we parents are wiser, and we probably often know exactly what the rules ought to be. But, if we'll take the time to let the kids have some input into those rules, they'll probably adhere to them much better than they would otherwise.

The "I've-Got-a-Banana-in-My-Ear" Game

This is the game played by children who can't seem to hear anything their parents tell them. As in, "You called me to dinner? Gee, mom, I'm sorry I didn't hear you. You see, I have these bananas stuck in my ears."

Parents who are successful at beating this game are the ones who learn to tell their children something *only one time*. Give them the *responsibility* of hearing you the first time. If they don't respond, just proceed as if they heard you. If he doesn't come to dinner when he's called your child will have to suffer the consequences—eating a very cold dinner, or going without altogether.

Not long ago, while driving in an area where roadwork was being done, I noticed a sign, "Warning! Left lane ends, one mile ahead." And still, people in the left lane kept sailing along. Another sign a bit further along read, "Warning! Left lane ends, 1,000 feet ahead." At this point a few of the drivers in the left lane began moving to the right, but most didn't. Finally we got to the point where the lane ended. Guess what happened?

That's right. All those cars in the left lane—and there were dozens of them—had to get into the right lane immediately. The result was a nifty little traffic jam. If they had started getting over after reading the first sign, traffic would have been able to move through the construction area fairly smoothly. But because those drivers waited until the third warning, they created problems for themselves and other motorists. I wonder how many of them learned to play the, "I've-got-a-banana-in-my-ear" game when they were children?

A good friend of mine always had a difficult time hearing the alarm clock in his own home. During their 25-year marriage, his wife always heard the alarm, got up, and then woke her husband. When he was on the road traveling, though, he was always awakened by his little portable alarm clock. In fact, he usually woke up right before the alarm went off. Why couldn't he do that at home? He was demonstrating the truth that *we can let other people be responsible for us*. If your children play the "banana" game, they need to be re-trained and made to understand that from now on, you will tell them something *only once*. And they had better learn to listen carefully!

The Hey-Look-Me-Over Game

It may be his hair. It may be a dress she wants to wear to a party. It may be a negative attitude toward something the parent holds dear. Whatever it is, it's designed to provoke the parents into confrontation. What can you do about it? The best thing is not to blow a fuse, but to keep quiet, and perhaps breathe a prayer that this particular style doesn't last very long!

Jim, age 16, surprised his mother one day by announcing he was quitting school. His mom, a single parent, was also a schoolteacher. She had always stressed the importance of education. This time, however, she resisted the initial temptation to lecture or scold him for his decision.

I told her it appeared her son was trying to hit her where it hurt. I also told her there was no way she could stop Jim from quitting school and that, in fact, his dropping out might really be an education for him. And, sure enough, it was. For 18 months he worked as a carpenter's apprentice in the "real world."

After working for that year-and-a-half he quit his job, enrolled in a local community college where he did better than average academically, and later transferred to a university. Jim learned a valuable lesson because his mother had the courage to let him make the decision that would affect his education and his life.

The Nobody-Likes-Me Game

Sometimes children will play a game designed to get parents to falsely praise them. *Responding to what the child says* is the greatest way to escape the jaws of this particular game.

Little Egmont comes in and says, "Oh, mom, I'm so ugly." This remark is intended specifically for the parent to say, "Oh, no you're not. You're a handsome boy!" But why put Egmont and his mother through this hassle? A simple statement such as, "I'm sorry you see yourself that way," might be truly helpful, without playing off the boy's negative comments about himself. On the other hand, if a child continually makes negative remarks about himself, or seems to have particularly poor self esteem, it may indicate professional help is needed.

The Never-Never Game

"You *never* let me spend the night at Billy's house!"
"We *never* have fried chicken for dinner!"
"I *never* get to go with my friends to the mall!"
All of these statements are variations on the same theme, the world-famous "Never-never game."

The best response to the invitation to play this game is to not respond at all. The child is exaggerating, and he or she knows it. Why recount all the times you've let him spend the

If Alan doesn't want to eat his beef stew because you *never* fix fried chicken, you might get out a piece of paper and write, "Tuesday, fried chicken for Alan." That ought to make him feel special and take some of the wind out of his sails at the same time. Chances are he'll settle down and eat his beef stew. If he still won't eat it, however, his dinner should be removed after a reasonable time without any nagging. If Alan gets hungry later on, that's merely the result of his decision not to eat.

Now don't think all the games children and their parents play originate with the children. Some games, just as harmful to the parent-child relationship, are instigated by the parents.

These games reflect the fact that many parents rely upon "traditional" methods of child-rearing. These methods assume parents are "better" than children, in the sense that they have to be superior in order to mete out punishment or pass down rewards. I've never found that to be the case. As a Christian parent I feel God loves us each the same—children and parents alike. We are unique individuals with different responsibilities, but we are equally important as human beings. What are some of the games parents like to play?

The Rubber Ball Game

Here's how this game works.
"Dad, can I go to the park to play?"
"Oh...why don't you go ask your mother?"
"Okay. Hey, mom, can I go to the park?"
"You have to ask your father."
"I already did."
"And what did he say?"
"He said to ask you."
What's going on here? Neither parent wants to make the decision. Dad's afraid that if he says yes, his wife might be

angry with him because she didn't think it was a good idea. Or, maybe dad doesn't think it's a good idea himself, but he's afraid to say no.

Whatever the reason, the child winds up feeling like a rubber ball being bounced between his parents. This game can be dispensed with if parents will communicate with each other regarding what is appropriate and not appropriate for their children. Parents must resolve to quit passing the buck, and make decisions based on communication.

I personally feel that when in doubt, it's always better to say no. It's easier to change a no to a yes than it is to change a yes to a no. Also, when you give a child a blanket yes to a question such as, "Mom, can we go to the ball game on Saturday, and have a picnic in the park afterward?" you're guaranteeing to the child that each member of the family will be well enough to attend, that the weather will be satisfactory, and that the car will be in proper working order. Because you have no control over these factors, a better response is, "We'll see what tomorrow brings." It sounds evasive and mysterious I know, but you should avoid making promises you may not be able to keep.

The Manners Game

One of the most humiliating games is the Manners Game, in which parents embarrass their children in front of others. For example, here is 4-year-old Krissy, who's just been given a present for her birthday. Like most 4-year-olds, she'll begin to rip open the package immediately. But before she gets very far into the process, mom says, "Krissy...what do you say to Mrs. Anderson? What do we say to people when they give us a present, honey?" Little Krissy shrugs her shoulders and withdraws, but mom persists, "Come on, honey...what should you say?"

Mrs. Anderson? What do we say to people when they give us a present, honey?" Little Krissy shrugs her shoulders and withdraws, but mom persists, "Come on, honey . . . what should you say?"

Now my point isn't that it's wrong to teach children to say thank you. Far from it. But in her attempt to teach manners, this mother is being disrespectful to her child. Yes, she is embarrassed, but so is her little girl, and needlessly so.

I believe a parent could handle a situation like this in a way that avoids embarrassing the child, even as it holds her accountable for saying thank you. One way would be to take possession of the gift until the child has thanked the giver. This thanks could be expressed by telephone at a later time, or by writing and sending a thank you card. What I'm saying is that it's good and important to teach your children manners, but there's no reason to embarrass them in front of others while you're doing it.

I've often wondered what would happen if parents ever treated company in their home the way they treat their children. Picture mom turning to one of her friends from church and asking, "Did you wash your hands before you came to the table?" Or, "Did you comb your hair before you sat down? It's a mess!" Why do so many parents feel comfortable about making those types of statements to their family members, but would never dream of doing the same thing to their guests? Someone once said we need to treat family as company and company as family, and I think that's a dandy idea.

The Treat-em-All-the-Same Game

Most parents assume they're being good parents when they treat all the children the same. Nothing could be further from the truth.

We pay a great deal of lip service in this country to the idea of allowing and supporting individual differences. I find that for the most part, however, we're intolerant of them. We can accept the fact that one 12-year-old is eight inches taller than another one, but we still expect all children to learn to read at the same speed, or else walk, talk, or achieve in the same manner. If they don't, we have a difficult time dealing with them. School systems, for instance, are generally designed to expect all the children of the same age to achieve at the same level. Parents may do the same thing.

We do our children a great disservice by expecting them all to be just alike, little cookies from the same cutter. They will demonstrate differences in temperament, personality and, more importantly, in strengths. What's important is to discover those individual strengths, and encourage and support your children in them.

Children do not like to be treated the same. They prefer to be treated differently because they are uniquely different people. They have different ages, different responsibilities, and different constitutions. Many times in our attempts to treat everyone the same, we really end up defeating a child. One of the things I'm most thankful for in my life is that my parents told me what they thought about certain situations and ideas, but always let me make my own choices. That is really the pinnacle of respect. It's important that parents respect the differences in children in this way.

I remember a couple who came up to me one night after a seminar. They shared that in the last few months, at ages 38 and 36, they had found God had a purpose and a plan for their lives. Their question was, "Okay, now that we have experienced the love of Christ, how do we get our teenage children to experience the same thing?"

I looked them straight on and said, "It's taken you 36 and 38 years to get to the place where you've turned your life over to God. Why are you demanding your children turn things around right now?

"God loves them just as he loved you. He loves them enough to give them opportunity to fail, to fall flat on their faces. He loves them enough to give them the right to reject Him if they choose. One of the things you can do is to pray for your children and pray for yourselves. You can be models in your home without even implying, 'Hey, children, be like us.' Each member of God's kingdom is unique, so you really don't want them to be just like you. It may take them a shorter period of time than it took you to come to terms with things in their lives, or it might take longer for them to commit themselves to God's love. Go on and live your lives together as you see fit. Then, with your loving relationship and the change that's occurred in your life, there ought to be plenty of evidence that God is real. That ought to provide a challenge for your children."

Dad spoke up and said, "Thanks, I think we needed to hear that." Because of their newness in Christ they were extremely anxious for their children to share the same joy. But God works at His own pace and in His own time.

Again, keep in mind that all of the games we've mentioned, whether they are initiated by the parent or child, must have cooperation from the opposition in order to be "successful." If one side or the other refuses to play, the game's over.

When a young couple begins to fight in my office, I'll listen to them for a short while and then say, "One thing I notice about you two is that you really do cooperate." They always seem startled that I see their fighting as an expression of cooperation. Yet when you think about it, that's what it is. It takes two people to fight and it takes two people—or two sides—to play games.

As a parent, watch out for the traps your children lay for you, and be careful not to walk into them. At the same time, be mindful of the games parents tend to play.

We've only touched on a few of these kinds of games here. There are countless numbers of them—and you can probably think of many others. Whatever they may be, do your best to stay out of them.

At the same time, give yourself the right to fail once in awhile. I guarantee you, it will happen. And give your children the right to fail, too. After all, they're only human.

God always gives us the right to fail. He loves us in spite of our flaws and shortcomings. Because that's the case, we can certainly turn around and love and accept our children in the same way.

Exercises

• What parent-child "games" can you think of that have not been covered in this chapter? Make a list of the ones you often get "suckered" into playing, as well as some steps you will take to avoid playing them in the future. (Once you recognize the games, it's easier to avoid them.)

• Spend some time talking to your spouse so that you have a "contingency plan" for dealing with the children. If you know beforehand what you would do in particular situations, then you are not likely to be manipulated into being pitted against each other. For example, do you know what disciplinary actions you would impose for certain infractions of family rules? If your child wanted to spend the night at a friend's house (as an example), would you be inclined to let him go if there was no reason not to? What if he wanted to have a friend spend the night at your house? If you have anticipated how you will handle specific circumstances, you will be much better off than if you just "fly by the seat of your pants."

10

Help,
I've Got Teenagers!

*T*he haggard-looking woman stood quietly off to the side while several other people crowded around, asking my advice on various matters pertaining to the raising of children. I had just finished a seminar on child-rearing, and I knew she wanted to ask me something. Yet whenever I looked over at her, she averted her eyes. It seemed she was struggling to gather the courage to say whatever was on her mind.

Finally, after everyone else had drifted away, she approached me. Clearing her throat, she said, "Dr. Leman... I really enjoyed what you said tonight. But I don't think any of it applied to me."

"Really?" I asked. "Why not?"

"Because, well..." she paused for a moment, as if searching for the words. "Because I've got... teenagers!"

Teenagers! People are supposed to run screaming at the mere mention of the word. And many do—especially those who have guided their own children through the teenage years. Make no mistake about this fact: it's always been difficult to help a child navigate the teenage years. However it has become even more difficult in the world of today.

This is an age that makes incredible demands on our children. They are pressured to experiment with drugs, and to get involved with sex as young as 11 or 12 years old. Everywhere they turn, the media bombards them with messages that are the antithesis of what we as Christian parents have tried to convey. What is a parent to do?

Well, let me tell you that it really *is* possible to get through to teenagers, even now. It *is* possible to overcome the influences of the world. And it *is* possible to get them to change their behavior and demonstrate a responsible approach to life. Granted, it may not be as easy as working with children of kindergarten age or younger, but it is possible to teach an old child some new tricks.

Now let me tell you that the woman I spoke with after the seminar had some real problems. Her two teenagers—a boy and a girl—were rebelling against her authority. She knew they were drinking and smoking, and she suspected their smoking wasn't limited to cigarettes. What made the situation even worse for her was that she was a Christian who had done her best to bring her children up in "the nurture and admonition of the Lord." She had taken them to church and Sunday school, she had prayed with them, and she had taught them many stories from the Bible. Yet they were beginning to act as if they'd spent their formative years riding around on the handlebars of a Harley.

The woman said she had always believed the Proverb that promises if you "train up a child in the way he should go, when he is old he will not depart from it" (Prov. 22:6). Now she was finding out it didn't always work out that way. Before we get any further into the specific problems faced by parents of teenagers, let me say two things about that verse in Proverbs.

1. It's generally true, but it's a principle rather than a hard-and-fast rule. There are times when even children of the most responsible Christian parents turn out to be—how can I phrase this delicately—rotten to the core. In the biblical book of 1 Samuel, you can read the story of Eli. He was a good man and a priest of Israel, but unfortunately his two sons, Hophni and Phinehas, were nothing more than common thugs.

2. The Proverb says, "when he is old" he will not depart from the way you've taught him. It doesn't say, "when he's a teenager." That's because when a child becomes an adolescent, he begins to kick against the limits of your authority, to find his own identity, to seek out new experiences. In many cases, this takes the form of rebellion. In some instances, it involves minor acts such as wearing the hair in a way you don't approve of or dressing in a way you don't particularly like. In other instances it is more extreme, including involvement in drugs and sex. But, if you can maintain a firm but loving attitude, it's almost certain that sooner or later your children will come back to your way of thinking.

In particular, I think of Sherry, who put her parents through absolute hell during her teenage years. Lesser parents might have thrown up their hands and said, "We give up. Just get out of our lives." But they stayed with it, and did their best to hold her responsible for her actions. They always let her know they loved her, even though they vehemently disapproved of what she was doing. And, just as important, they never stopped praying for her.

Well, Sherry and I have had some *interesting* discussions—believe me. Yet she made it through those rebellious days, and today is a responsible wife and mother of two pre-schoolers. She is also active in the PTA and the women's group at her church. She deeply regrets what she went through, especially because she hurt her parents so much. Because she was "trained in the way she should go," she has come back to it now that she is "old" (26).

I realize that some of what I've said so far might be discouraging, especially if you are the parent of a pre-teen. You might be thinking, "Does this mean I'm doomed to go through a period of rebellion with my child?" The answer to that is no, not necessarily.

But I do want you to know that if your teenager rebels against your authority, if he does things you wouldn't want him to do in a trillion years, that doesn't mean it's your fault. You as a parent are not responsible for your child's actions. The child, himself or herself, is responsible. A key to improving the situation is getting the child to face his responsibility, and to realize bad actions bring bad results. In order to maintain your sanity when dealing with a rebellious teenager, it is vitally important that you remember two things. They are:

1. It's not your fault.
2. You *can* change things.

Now let's take a look at some of the specific problems faced by teenagers and their parents, and talk about how to handle them. First of all...

Modern Problem Number One: Sex

Let me tell you one very important fact about sex: It's fun.

If you don't know that, I feel sorry for you. Sex is fun because God designed it to be so. He also designed it to be part of an intimate communion between one man and one woman who have pledged their lives to each other in marriage. But it's still fun, and that's what gets many teenagers into deep, deep trouble. Magic Johnson's recent revelation makes this point profoundly real.

What does teenage sex cause? It causes psychological problems. It causes unwanted pregnancy, even in these days of easily available birth control—and that means that it also causes abortion. It causes venereal disease. It causes AIDS, which always leads to death. And let me tell you something about AIDS. The "experts" talk about safe sex, and stress the use of condoms. But giving kids a device that isn't 100 percent effective to fight a disease that is 100 percent fatal is like giving them squirt guns to fight a raging forest fire. There is one cure for AIDS, and that's abstinence.

Another thing about sex is that there is extreme peer pressure to "do it." It used to be that peer pressure in this realm was the boys' domain, but not any more.

I talked to a 13-year-old girl, the daughter of Christian parents, who had become sexually active. When I asked her why she rolled her eyes and said, "Come on. *Nobody* wants to be a virgin!"

In her school, if you were a virgin you were a nerd. That's an attitude that parents have to fight. It's not nerdish, for boys or girls, to save themselves for marriage.

Now that we've recognized sex is fun and that there's terrific peer pressure to experiment with it, what can parents do to teach their kids to be responsible in this area? The best thing you can do is *talk to your kids about sex. It may be awkward at first, but you can* do it. Some parents hand their adolescent child a book about sex and say something like, "Let me know if you have any questions, feel free to call me at my toll free number at work!" That's certainly the coward's way out, and not very effective to boot.

179

What should you tell your child about sex?

1. That you understand his or her feelings. That the sex drive is extremely powerful, and that there is nothing shameful about thinking sexual thoughts. This is all a part of maturing as a human being.

2. That sex outside of marriage is wrong according to the Word of God. That your desire for him or her is to live in obedience to the Lord in this, as well as every other area of life. Not only is it wrong in the eyes of God, but it causes problems for both partners. It can lead to intense feelings of guilt and remorse.

3. That you're available to talk about any problems or questions regarding sex. Let your child know you're receptive and available, and that you will attempt to listen without judging.

4. That if he or she is determined to be sexually active, precautions must be taken to prevent unwanted pregnancy or worse. Not long ago, a distraught mother told me she had just discovered her 16-year-old daughter was taking birth control pills. I understood the mother's anguish. But, if the girl was going to be involved sexually, it is much better to be on the pill than to wind up pregnant. And, incidentally, I am certainly no fan of abortion, but it would do my heart good to see the church as a whole do as much for unwed mothers as it does to stop abortions. I believe this is an area where we as Christians fall far short of the mark.

5. I also believe parents of teenage boys need to stress that girls are worthy of honor and respect. They are not toys to be used and discarded. It may sound old fashioned, but a boy should be taught to treat a girl "like a lady." Take a look at how he relates to the women in his life—his mother, sisters, teachers, aunts, etc. If he doesn't treat them with honor and respect, then he needs a good talking to—hopefully from a

father who can demonstrate the proper attitude toward women.

The best thing parents can do for their teenagers is to demonstrate a healthy, loving relationship as husband and wife. If mom and dad love and respect each other, the kids will be more apt to understand what love and sex are all about.

Beyond that, the next-best thing is to be as open as possible about sex, and to realize it is a gift from God rather than a temptation from Satan. We get into trouble when we have a repressive attitude about sex. Trying to "keep the lid" on it is like trying to put toothpaste back in a tube. It's darn near impossible.

One of the areas where I believe repression can hurt more than expression is when it comes to masturbation. Studies I have seen suggest more than 90 percent of all adolescents masturbate—boys and girls.

I may lose a few readers here, but I don't see anything wrong with it. I would rather see a child participate in masturbation than get involved in casual sex with the boy or girl next door. When a parent comes to me and says, "What am I going to do? I just know my little Rodney has been masturbating," I say, "You can quit worrying about it. That's what you can do."

Modern Problem Number Two: Drugs

When I talk about drugs, I'm referring to everything from cigarettes to beer to crack cocaine. Not long ago, I even talked to a young man who told me he and his friends got high by inhaling the freon from his neighbor's heat pump.

Experts say drug use among high school and college students is decreasing, but I don't think we ought to be rejoicing yet. Drug use is still epidemic. It's still destroying the lives of thousands of young men and women every year.

Is your child on drugs? If you make the unfortunate discovery that he is, you're likely to react in one of the following unproductive ways:

1. Become hysterical.
2. Lecture.
3. Talk down to him.

I know it's hard in a situation like this, but the key here, as in every other aspect of dealing with today's teenagers, is to remain calm and rational. You need to communicate with your child on as equal a footing as possible.

Yes, you are the parent and he is the child. Yes, you are the one in authority. But this is an instance in which you must communicate your disapproval of the actions without disapproving of the child. If you suspect he is a chronic drug user, then by all means seek professional help. Otherwise, the best thing you can do is let him know if he persists in using drugs, you will not bail him out of whatever difficulty he finds himself in. In other words, you must make him responsible.

Are you knowledgeable about drugs? As a parent you ought to be. And because drug dealers are invading our grammar schools, it's never too early to talk to your kids about the dangers of drugs. There's no need to tell them horror stories and scare them half to death. The truth is scary enough. If a child has been forewarned about the dangers of drugs, he is not so likely to fall into that trap when it's sprung on him.

If you're not talking to your kids about drugs, you'd better start. The fact is, drugs are available to them whether you live in a major city or a tiny country town. If you're a Christian, show your children what God's Word says about harming the body.

If you have established the fact that you are able to talk with your children about anything—including drugs—then you've gone a long way toward winning the battle. If you've never had much success when it comes to communication, make up your mind to change. Sit the child down and say, "I know we haven't had much communication between us lately, but I really do want to try. I want to be here for you when you need someone to talk to. I promise I'll listen. And if you have any questions I can answer, I'd be happy to do so."

You may feel awkward having a conversation like that, but you've got to start somewhere. If your follow-up actions demonstrate you mean what you say, you can look for improvement in your relationship with your teenager.

Remember, communication is the best weapon in the fight against drugs.

Modern Problem Number Three: Depression

Why are kids so depressed these days? They've got it better than we had it when we were kids, don't they? Yet the suicide rate among teenagers is phenomenally high, everywhere in the United States.

Let me tell you, first of all, that today's kids don't have it better than we did, for many reasons. One of those reasons is that we're putting too much pressure on them. We want them to achieve something and be somebody. In far too many instances, we've tied our approval of them to their "success" in life. Your child needs to know you love him and are proud of him, that you couldn't love him more or be prouder of him no matter what he did—even if he were elected President!

A second way today's kids have it worse than we did is that they face peer pressure to involve themselves in outrageously dangerous activities. We had peer pressure back in my generation. That's what caused me to smoke my first cigarette when I was 7 years old. But the peer pressure I faced was nothing compared to what kids deal with today, as each generation tries to push the limits a little further.

The third reason today's kids are worse off than the generations before them is that our country's spiritual values have weakened. I don't know why, but in much of society respect for religious matters, especially for the authority of the Word of God, has decreased significantly.

A child without spiritual values is like a boat adrift on the ocean without a sail. Too many kids today are being raised in a short-sighted, hedonistic manner. Parents try to keep them happy by giving them everything they could possibly want, but they don't give their kids what really counts—a spiritual foundation upon which to build their lives. The result is that many of today's teenagers are selfish, mean, and never satisfied with what they have. Parents are knocking themselves out trying to get their kids to like them, but a teenager doesn't need his parent to be his friend. He needs his parent to be his parent!

Your teenager needs to know there are eternal values in life that matter. He needs to have an understanding that he is someone who is precious in God's sight, and that no matter what else may happen in life, he can know God loves him very much. Is your teenager involved in church? Is he part of an active youth group? If not, he should be. Does he see God is important in your life? That, too, is vital.

I realize it's sometimes hard to tell if a teenager is severely depressed, or if he's simply being cool by giving vent to his teenage anger. (Almost every teenager goes through at least one period where he's preoccupied with the futility of life in general. If he has spiritual values, however, that period won't last very long.)

Here are some signs of severe depression:

1. Drastic changes in personal appearance, from good to bad.

2. Constant complaints of upset stomach, headache, backache, etc.

3. Inability to concentrate.

4. Dramatic and sudden shifts in the quality of school work.

5. Changes in attitudes and behaviors such as excessive sleeping, withdrawal, decreased appetite, and emotional outbursts.

Can your child talk to you about the way he feels? If he tells you he's depressed, will you simply tell him to "snap out of it" and go on about your business? He doesn't need that sort of response. At the risk of sounding like a recording that plays over and over and over when one of the rides at Disneyland is out of commission, let me tell you again: What he needs, more than anything, is for you to take the time to talk to him. Actually, listen, more than talk.

I know it's scary to think about teenage suicide, but it's a fact of life. I believe we could go a long way toward preventing such tragedies if we would involve ourselves in our teens' lives and strive for honest and open communication. When we as parents are willing to share some of our deepest thoughts and feelings with our children, it enables them to share their deep concerns with us.

One of the things you can share with your depressed teenager is that there are almost always times during adolescence when life seems to be unbearable. But those times do not last. Teenage awkwardness and confusion give way to the grace and understanding of adulthood. Reassure your child that adolescence does not last forever, even though it sometimes seems that way!

"You mean, *you* felt this way, mom?"

"I sure did."

"Well, I can't believe that."

"Why can't you?"

"Because you're so together."

"Well, thanks. But not when I was your age. In fact, I didn't think I was going to live through it!"

A conversation like that one will go far toward improving a teenager's outlook on life. "Wow, mom had all these doubts and fears, too, and she turned out okay." Your child needs to see that you overcame, and so can he. However, if your child is obviously depressed and nothing you do seems to bring him out of it, then by all means, seek professional help.

Modern Problem Number Four: The Media

I recently heard on the news how police in New York City arrested a 9-year-old boy after he fired several rounds from a semi-automatic weapon into the wall of an office building. He told police he found the gun in a drawer at home. When they asked him how he knew how to load and reload it, he said, "I watch a lot of TV."

He is like most kids in the world today. Do you realize that an average 18-year-old has seen some 20,000 murders on television? No wonder so many of them are desensitized.

And, that's not all our kids are learning from the media.

You've probably heard about the battle over lyrics on records. The record companies have been pushed to include a "warning label" when lyrics are especially raunchy. Perhaps you've also heard about "2 Live Crew," a so-called musical group that seeks to cover up its incredible lack of talent with graphic sexuality and obscenity.

Any movie with a rating of worse than "PG" is going to be loaded with bad language and pay television has brought frontal nudity into most American homes. Now, four-letter words are starting to creep into prime-time network programming, and the glorification of pre- and extra-marital sex, along with the ridiculing of religion, is rampant.

It's not a good situation, and it's not getting better.

But, is censorship the answer? I don't think so. It simply is not possible to shelter your child from this aspect of life in our world. Does that mean I'd let your 6-year-old watch an R-rated movie? Of course not. However, you can't go around with him all the time, covering his eyes and ears whenever something happens that you don't want him to see or hear.

What, then, is the answer?

I believe it is to fight fire with fire. In other words, combat the sleaze, the filth, and the worldly with the good, the pure, and the eternal.

The Bible puts it this way: "Whatever things are true, whatever things are noble, whatever things are just, whatever things are pure, whatever things are lovely, whatever things are of good report, if there is any virtue and if there is anything praiseworthy—meditate on these things" (Phil. 4:8).

I trust you are making sure your child is exposed to the Word of God on a regular basis, and that he understands how God expects us to live. (As opposed to the lifestyle so much of the media is promoting.) I also strongly urge parents to expose their children to good, positive books, movies, plays, and music.

For instance, I love rock 'n' roll, but I'd much rather my kids were listening to Christian rockers like Petra and Stryper than unregenerate "artists" like Iron Maiden, Van Halen, or the aforementioned 2 Live Crew. And before you tell me Van Halen isn't so bad, let me remind you that the name of their recently released million-selling album was *For Unlawful Carnal Knowledge*. They should be ashamed of such childish crudity, and so should their record company. Anyway, my point is, instead of just saying, "I don't want you to listen to that stuff," encourage your child to discover rock music with a positive message. Take him to a Michael W. Smith concert, or buy him a cassette by a positive-oriented artist.

If you see a movie with your teen that offends you, talk about it. Start by asking what he thought of it. Then, without criticizing his response, let him know your reaction. For example, "Well, you know, I really didn't like that movie's approach to sex." In other words, encourage open communication in which you calmly explain your point of view. Refrain from saying things like, "That movie was a piece of trash, and here's why!" Communicate, don't preach!

Ten Rules for Parenting Teens Today

1. Be accepting. Don't tie your approval and acceptance to performance. Let your teen know you love and respect him just the way he is.

2. Take time to listen. If you find it's hard to just sit and talk to your teen, try changing the setting. Take him fishing for the day, or go horseback riding. Whatever you do, tell your teenager that you want to be available to him, that you value him as a person, and that you want to know what's on his mind. Simply taking the time to listen is one of the best things a parent can do, especially in these stress-filled times. Remember, if you don't listen to your teenager, he'll find someone else who will. That "someone else," however, might suggest solutions to your teen's problems that are far different from what you would offer.

3. Don't plan your teen's life for him. "Okay, Jimmy... here's your backpack, your lunch money and...oh, yes, the plan for your life. I've got it all drawn up, and all you have to do is follow it." If you've always wanted your daughter to be an actress and she seems more inclined to enter social work, do your best to be happy for her. It's her life. She has to live it the way she sees fit.

4. Be available. Is your teenager important to you? Then let him know it. Show him he's a top priority by being willing to drop whatever else you're doing when he needs your attention. When Billy comes in to talk to dad about something and dad doesn't even lower his eyes from the sports page, that does some damage to Billy's self-esteem. It also does some damage to his relationship with his father. And while I'm on this subject, I know you've heard it said that a woman's place is in the home. Well, I believe a man's place is in the home, too. He owes first allegiance to his wife and children, and he needs to demonstrate that fact over and over again.

5) Respect your teenager's privacy. Yes, you want to make sure your teen is staying out of trouble, but that's no reason to pry into his life unnecessarily. He needs to know you respect him as a human being enough to honor his need for privacy. Teenagers naturally need some time to be by themselves, and they may not be as inclined to talk to you as they were a few years ago. That's just the way it is. But, if you've always kept the lines of communication open, your kids will look for you when they need someone to talk to.

6. Share your real self. You're not helping your teenager if you foster the image that you were always a super-duper, A-1 kind of person. Have you ever experienced what he's going through now? Tell him about it. It will encourage him to know that you, too, have had to fight your way through this particular jungle.

7. Don't major on the minors. I think you know what I mean by this. Don't nag, or nit-pick, or concentrate on the relatively unimportant negatives in your teenager's life. If he's not perfect and he messes up every so often, it just goes to show that he's human. Try not to overreact. As you deal with your teenager constantly ask yourself, "Am I being *con*structive or *de*structive?" If you major on the minors you're being *de*structive, and it's time to change your approach.

8. Don't embarrass them. I know, this one is easier said than done. There's not a teenager anywhere who hasn't been embarrassed by his parents at one time or another. What I mean here is that you should avoid public displays of affection that would embarrass them. Also, don't yell at them in front of their friends, or call them cutesy nicknames. If there's anything a teenager resents it's being embarrassed in front of his friends. So remember that, and do your best to treat him like an adult—at least in front of his peers.

9. Ask for forgiveness when you need to. Have you treated your teenager shabbily in some way? Did you accuse him of lying, only to find out later he was telling the truth? Sooner or later, you're bound to make some mistakes with regard to your teenager. When that happens, the best thing you can do is say, "I'm sorry. I was wrong." Is it a sign of weakness to admit you goofed? Hardly! The truth is, it shows your teen you respect him enough to apologize. And it gives him more respect for you.

10. Remember you're a parent, not a "pal." While it's important to do everything within your power to keep the lines of communication open with your teenager, you must also make it clear you are the parent, not the "pal." I've counseled teens who told me their parents tried to dress like teenagers, talk like teenagers, and act like teenagers. How did

the kids feel about it? See Number 8. Your teenagers want your understanding and love, but they also want you to be their mom or dad, not their best buddy.

A Final Word of Encouragement

Parenting, whether your child is 18 months or 18 years, is the toughest job in the world. It always has been, and always will be. In fact, it seems to be getting tougher. But it can also be an exciting and fulfilling adventure if you have love, determination, and a well-developed sense of humor!

In conclusion, I just want to tell you: *I believe in you.* You're going to do just fine!

APPENDICES

APPENDIX I

A Child's
Ten Commandments

---

1. My hands are small, so please don't expect perfection when I make a bed, draw a picture, or throw a ball. My legs are short; please slow down so I can keep up with you.

2. My eyes have not seen the world as yours have, so please let me explore safely.

3. Please take the time to explain things to me about this wonderful world, and do so willingly.

4. My feelings are tender, so please be sensitive to my needs. Treat me as you would like to be treated.

5. Please treasure me as God intended you to do, holding me accountable for my actions, giving me guidelines to live by, and disciplining me in a loving manner.

6. Please go easy on the criticism, and remember that you can criticize the things I do without criticizing me.

7. Please give me the freedom to make decisions concerning myself, and even to fail, so I can learn from my mistakes.

---

8. Please don't do things over for me. That makes me feel my efforts didn't quite measure up to your expectations.

9. Mom and dad, show me that you love each other. That's something I need to know.

10. Don't forget to take me to Sunday school and church regularly. I enjoy learning about God, and I need to know He is my Friend.

APPENDIX II

———

Finding Professional Help

———

Throughout this book, I have made many references to seeking professional help when necessary. It may come to the point where you've done everything you know how to help your child, things haven't changed a bit, and you've run out of ideas. Don't despair. A good therapist can get through to a child who seems totally out of reach. The question is, how do you find a good therapist?

As a starting point, you need to ask the therapist some questions other than, "How much do you charge?" It used to be that whenever someone called to ask how much I charged for a counseling session, I'd tell him. Usually, he'd say, "Okay, thank you," and hang up. If he thought my rates were too expensive, I might never hear from him again. If he didn't he might make an appointment.

That kind of situation made me feel bad, because you shouldn't shop for a competent therapist the way you might shop for a new pair of pants or a blouse. So now whenever

———

someone calls to ask how much I charge I say, "I'll be happy to answer that question. Before I do, however, I think there are some other things you ought to ask about me. Questions like, 'What kind of a person are you? Are you married? Do you value marriage? Do you have any spiritual values? What is your training? Is there a particular model you follow in your therapy?'"

I realize we live in a money-oriented society, and that it might seem wise to shop around for a bargain. But when it comes to therapy, you want to find someone who can genuinely help you, not just someone who's going to give you a discounted rate. Now I'm not necessarily saying that the more you pay, the better help you'll get. Nor am I saying you should look for the therapist with the longest string of initials after his name, signifying all the degrees he has. What matters is the particular skills he or she possesses, along with his or her overall attitude about life.

For example, I have known Christians who have gone to non-Christian therapists and been told, in essence, that their problems related to their belief in God. If they could just get free from those "antiquated" ideas, and live the "liberated" life, they would be just fine. I've seen those kinds of therapists destroy lives with their ill-conceived suggestions and pseudo-therapy. Naturally, no believer would intentionally seek help from a person like that.

I'm not saying the therapist you choose has to be a Christian. But you should know, at least, that he is open to spiritual values and that he is not antagonistic toward those who seek to live the life of faith.

On the other hand, I have known people who went to well-meaning Christian therapists but received no real help because those therapists weren't equipped to handle the situation. In other words, there has to be more to the therapist you choose than simply the fact he is a Christian. After all, he can be a Christian and still be incompetent in other ways.

So...if there comes a time when you decide to seek professional help, please don't be afraid to ask questions before you sign up. If you can't get any answers, move on. And don't worry about asking a "dumb" question. There is no such thing when it comes to something this important.

Look for Someone Who Wants to Get Rid of You

When seeking a professional therapist, above all else, *look for someone who will try to get rid of you.* In other words, look for someone who is going to deal with you on as short a term as possible. Many counselors and psychologists feel no behavioral change can take place without a long-term committment—for example, one or two sessions per week for at least a year. I have not found this to be necessary. I believe that by locking a client into long-term therapy, we're saying he cannot handle his responsibilities and decisions in the real world.

I have known of many cases where people have gone to the same counselor for three, four years or more, without noticeable improvement. In such cases, you might almost say the patient has become "addicted" to therapy. He needs that session each week to "vent his feelings," by talking to someone who will listen. However, he isn't making any headway toward seeing the situation changed once and for all, and that's what therapy ought to be about.

If you are in doubt, and if a physician or pastor isn't available to refer you to a professional, call your State Board of Psychologists Examiners, or a local chapter of the American Association of Marriage and Family Counselors. They could at least provide you with a list of people who are certified professionals. This in no way certifies that the therapist is right for you, but it does protect you in the sense that all the people listed in the various associations have at least met minimum requirements. In some states, for instance, a person can call himself a counselor without any training or degree whatsoever. All he has to do is rent an office, hang out a shingle offering his counseling services, and he's in business.

Other Good
Harvest House Reading

TOO OLD, TOO SOON
by *Doug Fields*

Too Old, Too Soon examines the changes to childhood brought about by a culture caught in overdrive and offers concrete suggestions parents can use to avoid the pitfalls of rushing their children to adulthood.

RADICAL RESPECT
by *Jim Burns*

In a society permeated by sex and permissiveness, straight answers to questions about sexuality are still hard to come by. In *Radical Respect,* noted youth pastor Jim Burns balances straightforward discussion of real-life situations with God's original plan for sexuality.

SUCCESSFUL SINGLE PARENTING
by *Gary Richmond*

Author Gary Richmond offers practical help and suggestions to single parents in this valuable guide to successful single parenting. *Successful Single Parenting* provides answers to the toughest questions single parents face. Here is a resource of information and encouragement that parents can turn to again and again.

THE WORKING MOTHER'S GUIDE TO SANITY
by *Elsa Houtz*

Working mothers "have it all"—or do they? Written from a down-to-earth, practical perspective, *The Working Mother's Guide to Sanity* examines the most fundamental concerns and problems working mothers face.

Going beyond just identifying the problems, *The Working Mother's Guide to Sanity* provides answers, options, and solutions that work for the working mother.

TOO HURRIED TO LOVE
by *Charles Bradshaw* and *Dave Gilbert*

You know the feeling. . . . Your spouse is in shock when you remember a birthday. The kids can't believe it when you make it to their games. And it's been so long since you had coffee with friends that you've forgotten who your friends are! You're busy, but are you busy doing what matters? If it's time for midcourse corrections, this book will help. *Too Hurried to Love* is a "roadmap in a book" that will guide you to living with simplicity and purpose.

WHAT THEY NEVER TOLD US ABOUT HOW TO GET ALONG WITH EACH OTHER
by *Judson Edwards*

As we grow up, we discover a startling truth: People are fragile! We can hurt them. They can hurt us. Collisions are unavoidable, but they don't have to be miserable. We can learn to get along with each other—even when things aren't perfect. For people who are weary of stress in their interactions with others, *What They Never Told Us About How To Get Along With Each Other* points the way to quality relationships that last.

THE STAY-AT-HOME MOM
by *Donna Otto*

Applauding the stay-at-home mom, author Donna Otto takes on the challenges and highlights the rewards of staying at home. With boundless enthusiasm for home and personal organization, Otto cheers on the stay-at-home mom and provides practical ideas to make the journey an adventure. This book will help you know whether being a stay-at-home mom is right for *you*.

Dear Reader:

We would appreciate hearing from you regarding this Harvest House nonfiction book. It will enable us to continue to give you the best in Christian publishing.

1. What most influenced you to purchase *Getting the Best from Your Kids?*
   ☐ Author   ☐ Recommendations
   ☐ Subject matter   ☐ Cover/Title
   ☐ Backcover copy   ☐ _____

2. Where did you purchase this book?
   ☐ Christian bookstore   ☐ Grocery store
   ☐ General bookstore   ☐ Other
   ☐ Department store

3. Your overall rating of this book:
   ☐ Excellent   ☐ Very good   ☐ Good   ☐ Fair   ☐ Poor

4. How likely would you be to purchase other books by this author?
   ☐ Very likely   ☐ Not very likely
   ☐ Somewhat likely   ☐ Not at all

5. What types of books most interest you?
   (check all that apply)
   ☐ Women's Books   ☐ Fiction
   ☐ Marriage Books   ☐ Biographies
   ☐ Current Issues   ☐ Children's Books
   ☐ Self Help/Psychology   ☐ Youth Books
   ☐ Bible Studies   ☐ Other _____

6. Please check the box next to your age group.
   ☐ Under 18   ☐ 25-34   ☐ 45-54
   ☐ 18-24   ☐ 35-44   ☐ 55 and over

Mail to: Editorial Director
Harvest House Publishers
1075 Arrowsmith
Eugene, OR 97402

Name _____

Address _____

City _____ State _____ Zip _____

**Thank you for helping us to help you
in future publications!**